MICHIGAN COPTIC TEXTS

PAPYROLOGICA CASTROCTAVIANA

Studia et textus 7

directa a José O'Callaghan

GERALD M. BROWNE

MICHIGAN COPTIC TEXTS

PAPYROLOGICA CASTROCTAVIANA

BARCELONA

1979

TIPOGRAFIA DELLA PONTIFICIA UNIVERSITÀ GREGORIANA — ROMA

Contents

PREFACE

This edition of Coptic texts from the Michigan collection is the third in the series of volumes begun by W. H. Worrell and continued by E. M. Husselman.[1] In preparing it, I have derived great benefit from Dr. Husselman's description, in Worrell's volume (pp. 1-22), of the Michigan Coptic collection, as well as from her unpublished inventory.

The present publication contains texts — on papyrus, parchment, and paper — of a theological nature. They extend from the fourth to the eleventh centuries of our era. One piece (Number 2) was uncovered during the 1928/9 excavations of the University of Michigan at Karanis; the remainder were purchased by the University between 1920 and 1929. Of those purchased, at least two (Nos. 7 and 9), and possibly more, come from the celebrated library of the White Monastery, the source of many of the Coptic literary texts in the Michigan collection.[2]

---

[1] W. H. WORRELL, *Coptic Texts in the University of Michigan Collection* (Ann Arbor 1942); E. M. HUSSELMAN, *The Gospel of John in Fayumic Coptic* (*P. Mich. inv. 3521*) (Ann Arbor 1962). I list here the Michigan Coptic texts which I have published in periodicals:

Inv. 548: "The Martyrdom of Paese and Thecla," *Chronique d'Egypte* 49 (1974) 201-205.

Inv. 582a: "A Fragment of a Coptic Psalter," *The Bulletin of the American Society of Papyrologists* 12 (1975) 67-69.

Inv. 607: "The Sahidic Version of Kingdoms IV," *Illinois Classical Studies* 3 (1978) 196-206.

Inv. 6640: "A Coptic Letter from the Michigan Collection," *The Bulletin of the American Society of Papyrologists* 13 (1976) 89-91.

[2] See T. Orlandi, "Un projet milanais concernant les manuscrits coptes du Monastère Blanc," *Le Muséon* 85 (1972) 405.

Nos. 1-8 contain Coptic translations of the Bible; especially noteworthy are No. 2 (hitherto unidentified) and No. 6: they present important early witnesses to the Coptic Old and New Testaments and contribute to the study of dialectology. The rest of the volume includes the beginning of Gregory's Encomium on Basil (No. 9), a hymn to the archangel Michael (No. 10), a fragment from an early Bohairic text dealing with the archangel Raphael (No. 11), and two pieces which represent religion on a more vulgar level: one is an amulet (No. 12), the other a kind of almanac (No. 13).

Initially I studied the texts in this volume through photographs provided by a generous grant from the Research Board of the University of Illinois; later I was able to collate my transcripts autoptically with the originals in Ann Arbor. I am grateful to Dr. H. C. Jameson for permission to publish these pieces, and to my wife, Alma, who patiently studied some of the more intractable parts of this volume and made suggestions for their improvement. Above all, I owe thanks to Professor H. C. Youtie for all the help he has unstintingly given me through the years in understanding the meaning and application of editorial technique and textual criticism. It is to him that I dedicate *quidquid hoc libelli*.

1 August 1977

Urbana, Illinois

LIST OF ABBREVIATED TITLES

BUDGE, *Miscell. Texts* = E. A. WALLIS BUDGE, *Miscellaneous Coptic Texts in the Dialect of Upper Egypt* (London 1915).

BUDGE, *Psalter* = E. A. WALLIS BUDGE, *The Earliest Known Coptic Psalter* (London 1898).

BZ = *Byzantinische Zeitschrift*.

CCAG = *Catalogus Codicum Astrologorum Graecorum* (Brussels 1898-1953).

CIASCA, *Fragm. copto-sahid.* = A. CIASCA, *Sacrorum Bibliorum fragmenta copto-sahidica Musei Borgiani*. Vol. 2 (Rome 1889).

CRAMER, *Paläographie* = M. CRAMER, *Koptische Paläographie* (Wiesbaden 1964).

CRUM, *Dict.* = W. E. CRUM, *A Coptic Dictionary* (Oxford 1939).

DRESCHER, *Kingdoms I, II* = J. DRESCHER, *The Coptic (Sahidic) Version of Kingdoms I, II (Samuel I, II) (Corpus Scriptorum Christianorum Orientalium* 313 = Scriptores Coptici 35 [Textus], 314 = Scriptores Coptici 36 [Versio]; Louvain 1970).

GARITTE, *Vita Antonii* = G. GARITTE, *S. Antonii vitae versio sahidica (Corpus Scriptorum Christianorum Orientalium* 117 = Scriptores Coptici 13 [Textus]; Louvain 1967 [Reprint of edition of 1949]).

HORNER = [G. W. HORNER], *The Coptic Version of the New Testament in the Southern Dialect* (Oxford 1911-1924).

HORNER Boh. = [G. W. HORNER], *The Coptic Version of the New Testament in the Northern Dialect* (Oxford 1898-1905).

HUSSELMAN, *Gospel of John* = E. M. HUSSELMAN, *The Gospel of John in Fayumic Coptic (P. Mich. Inv. 3521)* (Kelsey Museum of Archaeology, Studies 2; Ann Arbor 1962).

JERNSTEDT, *Push.* = P. V. JERNSTEDT, *Koptskije Teksty Gosudarstvennogo Muzeya Izobrazitelnykh Iskusstv imeni A. S. Pushkina* (Moscow/Leningrad 1959).

JThS = *Journal of Theological Studies*.

JUNKER, *Koptische Poesie* = H. JUNKER, *Koptische Poesie des 10. Jahrhunderts*, in *Oriens Christianus* 6 (1906) 319-411 (I), 7 (1907) 136-253 (II), 8 (1911) 2-109 (III).

KAHLE, *Bala'izah* = P. E. KAHLE, *Bala'izah. Coptic Texts from Deir el-Bala'izah in Upper Egypt* (London 1954).

KASSER, *Compléments* = R. KASSER, *Compléments au Dictionnaire copte de Crum (Publications de l'Institut français d'Archéologie orientale. Bibliothèque d'études coptes* 7; Cairo 1964).

KASSER, *Compléments morphol.* = R. Kasser, *Compléments morphologiques au Dictionnaire de Crum*, in *Bulletin de l'Institut français d'Archéologie orientale* 64 (1966) 19-66.

KROPP, *Lobpreis* = A. M. KROPP, *Der Lobpreis des Erzengels Michael* (*vormals P. Heidelberg Inv. Nr. 1686*) (Brussels 1966).

KROPP, *Zaubertexte* = A. M. KROPP, *Ausgewählte koptische Zaubertexte* (Brussels 1930-1931).

LEIPOLDT, *Sinuthii vita bohairice* = J. LEIPOLDT, *Sinuthii vita bohairice* (*Corpus Scriptorum Christianorum Orientalium* 41 = Scriptores Coptici 1 [Textus]; Louvain 1951 [Reprint of edition of 1906]).

Leyd. = W. PLEYTE and P. A. A. BOESER, *Manuscrits coptes du Musée d'Antiquités des Pays-Bas à Leide* (Leiden 1897).

LSJ = H. G. LIDDELL, R. SCOTT, and H. S. JONES, *A Greek-English Lexicon* (Oxford 1940).

MPER = *Mitteilungen aus der Sammlung der Papyrus Erzherzog Rainer* (Vienna 1887-1897).

MURRAY, *Osireion at Abydos* = M. A. MURRAY, *The Osireion at Abydos* (*Publications of the British School of Archaeology in Egypt* 9; London 1904).

NAGEL, *Grammat. Untersuch.* = P. NAGEL, *Grammatische Untersuchungen zu Nag Hammadi Codex II*, in: F. ALTHEIM and R. STIEHL, *Die Araber in der Alten Welt* 5.2 (Berlin 1969) 393-469.

NH IV = *The Facsimile Edition of the Nag Hammadi Codices: Codex IV* (Leiden 1975).

OMH = E. STEFANSKI and M. LICHTHEIM, *Coptic Ostraca from Medinet Habu* (*University of Chicago, Oriental Institute Publications* 71; Chicago 1952).

ORLANDI, *Phif e Longino* = T. ORLANDI, *Vite dei monaci Phif e Longino* (*Testi e documenti per lo studio dell'antichità* 51; Milan 1975).

ORLANDI, *S. Mercurio* = T. ORLANDI, *Passione e miracoli di S. Mercurio* (*Testi e documenti per lo studio dell'antichità* 54; Milan 1976).

PG = J. P. MIGNE, *Patrologia Graeca* (Paris 1857-1866).

POLOTSKY, *Collected Papers* = H. J. POLOTSKY, *Collected Papers* (Jerusalem 1971).

POLOTSKY, *Conjugation System* = H. J. POLOTSKY, *The Coptic Conjugation System*, in *Orientalia* N.S. 29 (1960) 392-422.

POLOTSKY, *Coptic* = H. J. POLOTSKY, *Coptic*, in *Current Trends in Linguistics* 6: *Linguistics in South West Asia and North Africa* (The Hague 1970) 558-570.

POLOTSKY, *Études* = H. J. POLOTSKY, *Études de syntaxe copte* (Cairo 1944).

POLOTSKY, *Nominalsatz* = H. J. POLOTSKY, *Nominalsatz und Cleft Sentence im Koptischen*, in *Orientalia* N.S. 31 (1962) 413-430.

POLOTSKY, *Rev. Böhlig* = H. J. POLOTSKY, Review of A. Böhlig, *Der achmimische Proverbientext*, in *Orientalistische Literaturzeitung* 55 (1960) 23-27.

PORCHER, *Livre de Job* = E. PORCHER, *Le Livre de Job, version copte bohaïrique* (*Patrologia Orientalis* 18.2; Paris 1924).

Push. See Jernstedt, *Push.*

QUECKE, *P. Mil. Copti = Papiri della Università degli Studi di Milano (P. Mil. Copti), Volume Quinto*: *Lettere di San Paolo in Copto-Ossirinchita*: *Edizione, commento e indici di Tito Orlandi, Contributo linguistico di Hans Quecke* (Milan 1974).

RAHLFS, *Berliner Psalter* = A. RAHLFS, *Die Berliner Handschrift des sahidischen Psalters (Abhandlungen der Königlichen Gesellschaft der Wissenschaften zu Göttingen.* Philologisch-historische Klasse N.F. 4, No. 4; Berlin 1901).

REYMOND-BARNS, *Coluthus* = E. A. E. REYMOND and J. W. B. BARNS, *Four Martyrdoms from the Pierpont Morgan Coptic Codices* (Oxford 1973). (*Coluthus* is on pp. 25-29; translation, pp. 145-150.)

Ryl. = W. E. CRUM, *Catalogue of the Coptic Manuscripts in the Collection of the John Rylands Library, Manchester* (Manchester 1909).

SCHMIDT, *Clemensbrief* = C. SCHMIDT, *Der erste Clemensbrief in altkoptischer Übersetzung (Texte und Untersuchungen zur Geschichte der altchristlichen Literatur* 32.1; Leipzig 1908).

SCHUBART, *P. Graec. Berol.* = W. SCHUBART, *Papyri Graecae Berolinenses (Tabulae in usum scholarum* 2; Bonn 1911).

STEGEMANN, *Paläographie* = V. STEGEMANN, *Koptische Paläographie* (Heidelberg 1936).

THOMPSON = H. THOMPSON, *The Coptic Version of the Acts of the Apostles and the Pauline Epistles in the Sahidic Dialect* (Cambridge 1932).

TILL, *Achmim. Gramm.* = W. TILL, *Achmîmisch-koptische Grammatik* (Leipzig 1928).

TILL, *Bauernpraktik* = W. TILL, *Eine koptische Bauernpraktik*, in *Deutsches Institut für aegyptische Altertumskunde in Kairo, Mitteilungen* 6 (1936) 108-149; Nachtrag 175-176.

TILL, *Bemerkungen* = W. TILL, *Bemerkungen zu koptischen Textausgaben*, in *Orientalia* N.S. 12 (1943) 328-337.

TILL, *Dialektgramm.* = W. TILL, *Koptische Dialektgrammatik.* 2nd Edition (Munich 1961).

TILL, *Gramm.* = W. TILL, *Koptische Grammatik (Saïdischer Dialekt.* 3rd Edition (*Lehrbücher für das Studium der orientalischen und afrikanischen Sprachen* 1; Leipzig 1966).

TILL, *Wochentagsnamen* = W. TILL, *Die Wochentagsnamen im Koptischen*, in *Publications de l'Institut d'études orientales de la Bibliothèque Patriarcale d'Alexandrie* 2 (= *Tome commémoratif du millénaire de la Bibliothèque Patriarcale d'Alexandrie*; Alexandria 1953) 101-110.

TSBA = Transactions of the Society of Biblical Archaeology.

TUKI, *Rudimenta* = R. TUKI, *Rudimenta linguae coptae sive aegyptiacae* (Rome 1778).

TURNER, *Typology of the Codex* = E. G. TURNER, *Some Questions about the Typol-

ogy of the Codex, in *Akten des XIII. Internationalen Papyrologenkongresses* (= *Münchener Beiträge zur Papyrusforschung und antiken Rechtsgeschichte* 66; Munich 1974) 427-438.

WESSELY, *Sahidisch-griechische Psalmenfragmente* = C. WESSELY, *Sahidisch-griechische Psalmenfragmente* (*Sitzungsberichte der Kaiserlichen Akademie der Wissenschaften. Philosophisch-historische Klasse* 155.1; Vienna 1908).

WESTENDORF, *Handwörterbuch* = W. WESTENDORF, *Koptisches Handwörterbuch* (Heidelberg 1965ff).

WORRELL, *Mich.* = W. H. WORRELL, *Coptic Texts in the University of Michigan Collection* (*University of Michigan Studies: Humanistic Series* 46; Ann Arbor 1942).

WS = W. E. CRUM and H. I. BELL, *Wadi Sarga: Coptic and Greek Texts from the Excavations undertaken by the Byzantine Research Account* (= *Coptica* 3; Hauniae 1922).

ZAeS = *Zeitschrift für ägyptische Sprache und Altertumskunde.*

EDITORIAL PROCEDURES

I follow the principles observed in editing texts on papyrus, and the symbols have their conventional meaning: square brackets, [ ], indicate a lacuna, and angle brackets, < >, an omission in the original. Abbreviations, generally *nomina sacra*, are not resolved. Dots inside brackets represent the number of letters missing, dots outside brackets indicate illegible letters, and dots placed under letters mark them as uncertain.

In order to reproduce the texts as closely as possible, I have introduced only word division in my transcriptions. Orthographic and grammatical peculiarities have been allowed to stand; where they can occasion confusion, I add a note in the commentary accompanying each piece. As regards supralinear marks — both strokes and points —, printing requirements have necessitated two deviations from absolutely accurate reproduction: 1) strokes or points between two letters on the original are set over the second in the transcript; similarly, long lines over three letters are centered over the second;[1] 2) for late texts, where supralinear strokes may be considerably shortened so as at times to be hardly distinguishable from points, it would be ideal to have a series of strokes of different lengths; in the absence of this ideal, I have had to decide, rather arbitrarily at times, whether a stroke or a point should be printed. Fortunately, the photographs included in this volume will allow the reader to judge the extent of my arbitrariness.

In my collations with biblical texts I exclude minor orthographic variations, and whenever I collate a piece with H(orner) and Th(ompson), I list only the readings which differ from those two editions; variants in the apparatuses of H and Th (designated as H^{app} and Th^{app}, respectively) are not cited except where they agree with the reading of the Michigan text.

Throughout this volume I use R(ecto) and V(erso) without any codicological significance. They are merely convenient designations of the first and second side, respectively, of the text under discussion.

---

[1] Note, however, that in the case of *nomina sacra*, the edition maintains the stroke over two or three letters.

TABLE OF TEXTS

1

PSALM 115 (116) 3-7

P. Mich. inv. 3589   16.6 × 10 cm.   6th or 7th cent.

This text is described as follows in Worrell, *Mich.* pp. 9f: "Papyrus fragment, broken off on the left and at the top, with text on the recto only. On the verso, at right angles to the text on the recto, are the words ѰΑ]ΛΜΟϹ ΜΠΧΟΕΙϹ .[, which are apparently the title." On the recto, the writing is across the fibers.

Written in large, clear letters, the Michigan piece may be for use in the service. It is difficult to date the text accurately, because so little remains, but I should prefer to assign it to the sixth or seventh century: it resembles Cramer, *Paläographie* Nos. 15 and 16 (6th-7th cent.) and is slightly more stylized than the former and not as well executed as the latter.

Hitherto, as far as I have been able to ascertain, only two texts with this part of Psalms have appeared: Budge, *Psalter*, and Wessely, *Sahidisch-griechische Psalmenfragmente* 55-57. Below the transcription of the Michigan text, I provide a collation of these two witnesses, designated as L and V, respectively.[1]

---

[1] There is also a citation from verse 3 in TUKI, *Rudimenta* 217, cited in CIASCA, *Fragm. copto-sahid.* II 145: ΕΙΝΑΤΕΕΒ ΟΥ ΜΠΧΟΕΙϹ ΕΠΜΑ ΝΝΕΝΤΑЧΑΑΥ ΝΑΙ ΤΗΡΟΥ. (For the source of the citations in Tuki, see RAHLFS, *Berliner Psalter* 7 and n. 1.)

↑　　　　　　　　　　　Ṇ]ẠІ [ΤΗΡΟΥ †ΝΑΧΙ ΝΟΥ] 115 (116) 3, 4

[ΧШ ΝΟΥΧΑΙ ΤΑΕΠ]ΪΚΑΛΕΙ ΜΠΡΑΝ ΜΠ[ΧΟΕΙϹ]

[ΠΜΟΥ ΝΝΕΤΟΥΑΑΒ] ΜΠΧΟΕΙϹ ΤΑΪΗΥ ΜΠΕЧΕΜ　　　　　5

[ΤΟ ΕΒΟΛ Ш ΠΧΟΕΙϹ] ΑΝΟΚ ΠΕ ΠΕΚΖΜΖΑΛ　　　　　6

5　[ΑΝΟΚ ΠΕ ΠШΗΡΕ Ν]ΤΕΚΖΜΖΑΛ ΑΚϹШΛП ΝΝΑ

[ΜΡΡΕ †ΝΑШШТ ΝΑΚ] ΝΝΟΥΘΥϹΙΑ ΝϹΜΟΥ　　　　　7

[†ΝΑ† ΝΝΑΕΡΗΤ ΜΠ]ΧΟΕΙϹ ΖΝ ΝΑΥΛΗ ΜΠΗΪ

[ΜΠΕΝΝΟΥΤΕ ΜΠΕΜ]ΤΟ ΕΒΟΛ ΜΠΛΑΟϹ ΤΗΡϤ

[ΖΝ ΤΟΥΜΗΤΕ ΘΙΛΗ]Μ ＞ ＞ ＞ ＞ ＞ ＞ ＞ ＞ ＞ ＞

　　　　　　　　　　]——————————————

Collation with L and V

vs. 4 ΤΑΕΠΙΚΑΛΕΙ L: ΝΤΑШШ ΕΒΟΛ V　　　6 ΑΝΟΚ ΠΕ (bis): ΑΝΓ L, ΑΝΟΚ V
7 †ΝΑШШТ L: †ΝΑШШТ V　　　ΝΝΟΥΘΥϹΙΑ: ΝΟΥΘΥϹΙΑ LV ΘΙΛΗΜ L: ΘΙΕΡΟΥ-
ϹΑΛΗΜ V

　　5 (vs. 6) The lacuna is restored on the basis of ΑΝΟΚ ΠΕ ΠΕΚΖΜΖΑΛ in the
preceding line.　Neither ΑΝΓ (L) nor ΑΝΟΚ (V) suits the space available.
　　9 (vs. 7) There is no room for the reading of V, ΘΙΕΡΟΥϹΑΛΗΜ.

2

JOB 30.21-30

P. Mich. inv. 5421　　　　　10.5 × 9.1 cm.　　　　　4th or 5th cent.

　　This papyrus, a fragmentary leaf from a codex, was acquired by the
University of Michigan in the 1928/9 excavations at Karanis.　The
sheet is broken off on three sides; the recto (11 lines of writing) preserves
the right margin, the verso (10 lines) the left.　Due to the absence
of close parallels, we cannot determine precisely how much text is lost

between the end of the recto and the beginning of the verso; but the amount cannot have been great, and probably did not exceed three lines. After restoration, the average line length is 11.5 cm. The extant margin is ca. 1.3 cm., and the original breadth of the sheet was probably about 14 cm. Although the upper and lower margins do not survive, a rough calculation based on the amount of text presumed lost suggests that, when intact, the sheet was approximately 14 cm. high. We are therefore dealing with the smaller square format found in such early Coptic codices as the *Gespräche Jesu*, the *Mississippi Crosby*, and the *Achmimic Proverbs*.[1]

Both codex typology and individual letter forms[2] place the text early, probably in the fourth or early fifth century, but I have been unsuccessful in finding a close parallel to the overall style of writing.

Related to the early date is the absence of dialect standardization. What remains often has a vocalization associated with Fayumic: NEI R 3 (Sah. NA), EMKE2 5 (S. MKA2), 4NEMANKT 6 (S. 4NAMONKT), KE2I 8 (S. KA2), 2H 11 (S. 2E). Certain elements, however, suggest Oxyrhynchite: note especially the lack of lambdacism and of doubled vowels (ЩEP V 9: S. ЩAAP) and the presence of 2A- as a conjugation base of the Perfect I (though in seemingly free alternation with A-).[3] Final unaccented -I instead of Oxyrhynchite -E[4] (e.g. ЩПI V 4) points again towards Fayumic, if not Bohairic, for the text does not lack an occasional Bohairicism: NETMЩ[OYT] R 7f, O]YON ЩXOM 9, NATXA PЩ4 V 5. Non-Fayumic features appear also in such forms as MMOI R 4, 9, instead of MMAI, AYTA2OI V 3, instead of AYTA2AI. Confronted with this dialectal fluidity, the editor cannot hope to achieve certain restoration, even in short lacunae, and I have contented myself with

---

[1] For the small format, see TURNER, *Typology of the Codex* 437.

[2] The most noteworthy appears to be the Щ with its angular tail: see HUSSELMAN, *Gospel of John* 42 n. 9. A similar Щ occurs in *NH* IV, e.g. 39.5.

[3] See QUECKE, *P. Mil. Copti* 97 (lack of lambdacism in Ox.), 90 and n. 30 (absence of doubled vowels), and 105 and n. 183 (2A-). 2A- and A- also alternate in P. Mich. inv. 3520 ined. (HUSSELMAN, *Gospel of John* 43 n. 18).

[4] QUECKE, *P. Mil. Copti* 91.

purely exempli-gratia reconstructions; in the commentary I suggest
alternative possibilities.

Especially noteworthy are the Bohairicisms; they can be explained
on the assumption that the author was copying from a Bohairic original
and neglected at times to make the necessary adjustments. But it is
also possible that we are dealing with a Bohairic scribe who failed completely to suppress his native dialect.

Compared with the Sahidic and Bohairic versions,[5] the Michigan
papyrus shows a slight tendency to agree with the latter; but there are
numerous discrepancies, as will easily be seen from an examination
of the two versions, which I print below the transcript and translation
of the Michigan text.

The only diacritical mark is a high dot set between the ⲁ and ⲧ
in ⲚⲀⲦⲬⲀ ⲢⲰϤ in V 5. The verso contains points in the margin,
placed opposite each line to guide the scribe.

Recto

— — — — — — — — — — — — — — — — —

→   [˙   ] · [

       [˙   ⲌⲈⲚ] ⲞⲨⲬⲒⲬ Ⲉ[Ⲥ]   30.21

       [˙ ⲬⲀⲢ ⲌⲈ]Ⲛ Ⲟ[ⲨⲘⲈⲦ]ⲀⲦⲚⲈⲒ Ⲁ

       [˙ ⲔⲈⲢ] ⲘⲀⲤⲦⲒⲄⲞⲒⲚ ⲘⲘⲞⲒ ⲀⲔ   22

    5 [˙ ⲦⲀ]ϢⲦ ⲌⲈⲚ ⲠⲈⲘⲔⲈⲌ ⲚⲌⲎ

       [˙ Ⲧ ⲦⲈⲒ]ⲘⲒ ⲬⲈ ϤⲚⲈⲘⲀⲚⲔⲦ Ⲛ   23

       [˙ ⲬⲈ Ⲡ]ⲘⲞⲨ ⲠⲎⲒ ⲄⲀⲢ ⲚⲚⲈⲦⲘϢ

       [˙ ⲞⲨⲦ] ⲦⲎⲢⲞⲨ ⲠⲈ ⲠⲔⲈⲌⲒ ⲌⲀⲘⲞⲒ   24

       [˙ ⲚⲈ Ⲟ]ⲨⲞⲚ ϢⲬⲞⲘ ⲘⲘⲞⲒ ⲚⲦⲀ

---

[5] Sahidic: Ciasca, *Fragm. copto-sahid.* II 48f (see also below, note to V 1-3, footnote 2); Bohairic: Porcher, *Livre de Job* 298f. Below each version I give the
significant manuscript variants; for identification of the manuscripts involved,
the reader is referred to the apparatus in each edition.

10   [˙ �glⲁⲧⲃ]ⲉ[ⲧ] ⲏ ⲛⲧⲁⲧⲱⲃⲅ ⲛⲕⲉ
     [˙ ⲟⲩⲉⲓ ⲛϥⲉⲓ]ⲣⲓ ⲛⲉⲓ ⲛⲧⲉⲓⲅⲏ ⲅⲁⲓ   25

(Ca. 3 lines missing)

Verso

↑   [˙ ..].ⲣⲉⲃ[   ]   26
   ˙ ⲛ ⲅⲉⲛⲅⲟⲟ[ⲩ   ]
   ˙ ⲁⲩⲧⲁⲅⲟⲓ ⲛ[ⲭⲉ ⲅ]ⲉⲛⲅⲟⲟ[ⲩ ⲉⲩⲅⲁ]
   ˙ ⲟⲩ ⲅⲁⲓϣⲱⲡⲓ ⲅⲉⲛ ⲟⲩ[ⲁϣ ⲁⲅ]   28
5 ˙ ⲟⲙ ⲛⲁⲧⲭⲁ ⲣⲱϥ ⲅⲁⲓⲟⲩ[ⲱⲅ]
   ˙ ⲅⲉⲛ ⲟⲩⲥⲩⲛⲁⲅⲱⲅⲏ ⲅ[ⲁⲓϣ]
   ˙ ϣ ⲉⲅⲣⲏⲓ ⲅⲁⲓⲉⲣ ϣⲃⲏⲣ [ⲉⲛⲓⲭⲓ]   29
   ˙ ⲣⲏⲟⲥ ⲛⲉⲙ ⲛⲓⲥⲧⲣⲟⲩ[ⲑⲟⲥ]
   ˙ ⲅⲁ ⲡⲁϣⲉⲣ ⲛⲉⲙ ⲛⲁⲕⲉ[ⲥ]   30
10 ˙ ⲭⲱⲭⲓ ⲉⲃⲟⲗ ⲙⲡⲕ[ⲁⲩⲙⲁ]

R

(30.21) ... with a strong hand, without pity you whipped me, (22) and
you set me in pain. (23) I know that death will destroy me, for the
home of all the dead is the earth. (24) Would that it were possible
for me to kill myself or to beg another to do so for me. (25) I ...

V

(26) ... days ... evil days befell me. (27 omitted) (28) I was in never-
silent sighing, I resided in an assembly, and I shouted. (29) I became
friends with the ostriches and the sparrows, (30) and my skin and my
bones became dark from the heat.

Bohairic Version (above, footnote 5)

(30.21) ⲀⲨⲦⲰⲞⲨⲚ ⲆⲈ ⲈⲌⲢⲎⲒ ⲈⲬⲰⲒ ⲊⲈⲚ ⲞⲨⲘⲈⲦⲀⲦⲚⲀⲒ ⲀⲔⲈⲢ ⲘⲀⲤⲦⲒⲄⲄⲞⲒⲚ ⲘⲘⲞⲒ ⲊⲈⲚ ⲞⲨⲬⲒⲬ ⲈⲤⲬⲞⲢ (22) ⲀⲔⲐⲀⲰⲦ ⲆⲈ ⲈⲌⲀⲚⲈⲘⲔⲀⲌ ⲚⲌⲎⲦ ⲞⲨⲞⲌ ⲀⲔⲂⲈⲢⲂⲰⲢⲦ ⲈⲂⲞⲖ ⲌⲀ ⲠⲒⲞⲨⲬⲀⲒ (23) ⲦⲈⲘⲒ ⲬⲈ ⲪⲘⲞⲨ ⲠⲈⲦⲚⲀⲘⲞⲨⲚⲔⲦ ⲠⲎⲒ ⲄⲀⲢ ⲚⲚⲒⲢⲈϤ-ⲘⲰⲞⲨⲦ ⲦⲎⲢⲞⲨ ⲠⲈ ⲠⲒⲔⲀⲌⲒ (24) ⲀⲘⲞⲒ ⲄⲀⲢ ⲚⲈ ⲞⲨⲞⲚ ⲮⲬⲞⲘ ⲘⲘⲞⲒ ⲠⲈ ⲈⲊⲞ-ⲐⲂⲈⲦ ⲘⲘⲀⲨⲀⲦ ⲒⲈ ⲚⲦⲀⲦ ⲌⲞ ⲈⲔⲈⲞⲨⲀⲒ ⲚⲦⲈϤⲈⲢ ⲪⲀⲒ ⲚⲎⲒ (25) ⲀⲚⲞⲔ ⲆⲈ ⲀⲒⲢⲒⲘⲒ ⲈⲬⲈⲚ ⲀⲦⲬⲞⲘ ⲚⲒⲂⲈⲚ ⲰⲀⲒϤⲒ ⲀⲌⲞⲘ ⲆⲈ ⲀⲒⲰⲀⲚⲚⲀⲨ ⲈⲞⲨⲢⲰⲘⲒ ⲊⲈⲚ ⲌⲀⲚⲀ-ⲚⲀⲄⲔⲎ (26) ⲈⲒⲬⲎ ⲀⲚⲞⲔ ⲊⲈⲚ ⲚⲒⲀⲄⲀⲐⲞⲚ ⲌⲎⲠⲠⲈ ⲀⲨⲒ ⲈⲌⲢⲎ ⲈⲬⲰⲒ ⲘⲀⲖⲖⲞⲚ ⲚⲬⲈ ⲌⲀⲚⲈⲌⲞⲞⲨ ⲚⲦⲈ ⲌⲀⲚⲠⲈⲦⲌⲰⲞⲨ (27 omitted) (28) ⲀⲒⲘⲞⲰⲒ ⲈⲒϤⲒ ⲀⲌⲞⲘ ⲚⲦⲬⲰ ⲚⲢⲰⲒ ⲀⲚ ⲀⲒⲞⲌⲒ ⲈⲢⲀⲦ ⲊⲈⲚ ⲞⲨⲞⲰⲞⲨⲦⲤ ⲈⲒⲰⲰ ⲈⲂⲞⲖ (29) ⲀⲒⲈⲢ ⲤⲞⲚ ⲈⲚⲒⲤⲎⲢⲎⲚⲞⲤ ⲞⲨⲞⲌ ⲚⲮⲪⲎⲢ ⲈⲚⲒⲤⲦⲢⲞⲨⲐⲞⲤ (30) ⲠⲀⲮⲀⲢ ⲀϤⲈⲢ ⲬⲀⲔⲒ ⲞⲨⲞⲌ ⲚⲀⲔⲀⲤ ⲈⲂⲞⲖ ⲊⲈⲚ ⲠⲔⲀⲨⲘⲀ

---

21 ⲀⲔⲦⲰⲞⲨⲚ

Sahidic Version (above, footnote 5)

(30.21) ⲀⲔⲈⲒ ⲈⲬⲰⲒ ⲌⲚ ⲞⲨⲘⲚⲦⲀⲦⲚⲀ ⲀⲔⲘⲀⲤⲦⲒⲄⲞⲨ ⲘⲘⲞⲒ ⲌⲚ ⲞⲨ6ⲒⲬ ⲈⲤⲬⲞⲞⲢ (22) ⲀⲔⲔⲰ ⲘⲘⲞⲒ ⲌⲚ ⲌⲈⲚⲌⲒⲤⲈ ⲀⲔⲚⲞⲬⲦ ⲈⲂⲞⲖ ⲘⲠⲞⲨⲬⲀⲒ (23) ⲦⲤⲞⲞⲨⲚ ⲄⲀⲢ ⲬⲈ ⲠⲘⲞⲨ ⲠⲈⲦⲚⲀⲞⲨⲞⲰⲦ ⲠⲎⲒ ⲄⲀⲢ ⲘⲠⲢⲰⲘⲈ ⲠⲈ ⲠⲔⲀⲌ (24) ⲌⲀⲘⲞⲒ ⲄⲀⲢ ⲈⲚⲈ ⲚⲦⲀⲒ6Ⲙ 6ⲞⲘ ⲈⲚ ⲘⲠⲀⲘⲞⲨ ⲚⲀⲒ Ⲏ ⲈⲤⲈⲠⲤ ⲔⲈⲞⲨⲀ ⲚϤⲢ ⲠⲀⲒ ⲚⲀⲒ (25) ⲀⲚⲞⲔ ⲆⲈ ⲀⲒⲢⲒⲘⲈ ⲈⲬⲚ 6ⲰⲂ ⲚⲒⲘ ⲀⲒⲀⲰ ⲀⲌⲞⲘ ⲆⲈ ⲚⲦⲈⲢⲒⲚⲀⲨ ⲈⲨⲢⲰⲘⲈ ⲌⲚ ⲚⲈϤⲀⲚⲀⲄⲔⲈ (26) ⲈⲒⲰⲞⲞⲠ ⲄⲀⲢ ⲌⲚ ⲚⲀⲀⲄⲀⲐⲞⲚ ⲈⲒⲤ ⲌⲎⲎⲦⲈ ⲆⲈ ⲀⲨⲦⲰⲘⲦ ⲈⲢⲞⲒ ⲈⲌⲞⲨⲈ ⲈⲢⲞ-ⲞⲨ Ⲛ6Ⲓ ⲌⲈⲚⲌⲞⲞⲨ ⲘⲠⲈⲐⲞⲞⲨ (27 omitted) (28) ⲀⲒⲘⲞⲞⲰⲈ ⲈⲒⲀⲰ ⲀⲌⲞⲘ ⲈⲬⲚ ⲔⲀⲢⲰⲒ ⲀⲒⲀⲌⲈ ⲆⲈ ⲀⲢⲀⲦ (sic) ⲌⲚ ⲞⲨⲘⲎⲎⲰⲈ ⲈⲒⲰⲰ ⲈⲂⲞⲖ (29) ⲀⲒⲢ ⲤⲞⲚ ⲚⲤⲈⲢⲎⲚⲞⲤ ⲀⲨⲰ ⲚⲰⲂⲎⲢ ⲈⲚⲈⲤⲦⲢⲞⲨⲐⲞⲤ (30) ⲀⲠⲀⲮⲀⲢ ⲆⲈ ⲔⲘⲞⲘ ⲈⲘⲀⲦⲈ ⲀⲨⲰ ⲚⲀⲔⲈⲈⲤ ⲈⲂⲞⲖ ⲌⲘ ⲠⲔⲀⲨⲘⲀ

---

21 ⲀⲔⲈⲒ ⲈⲌⲢⲀⲒ ⲈⲬⲰⲒ　　23 ⲘⲠⲢⲰⲘⲈ] ⲚⲢⲰⲘⲈ ⲚⲒⲘ　　24 ⲈⲚⲈ ⲚⲦⲀⲈϤ 6Ⲙ 6ⲞⲘ
ⲈⲚ ⲠⲘⲞⲨ ⲚⲀⲒ, om. Ⲏ　　26 ⲈⲒⲰⲞⲞⲠ ⲌⲰ ⲌⲚ ⲌⲈⲚⲀⲄⲀⲐⲞⲚ　　ⲈⲌⲞⲨⲈ ⲈⲢⲞⲞⲨ om.
et legit ⲈⲢⲞⲒ Ⲛ2Ⲛ2ⲞⲞⲨ　　28 ⲀⲬⲚ　　ⲀⲒⲀⲌⲈⲢⲀⲦ et om. ⲆⲈ　　29 ⲚⲚⲤⲈⲢⲒⲚⲞⲤ

R

　　1 Only a faint, unidentifiable trace remains.
　　2f ⲌⲈⲚ] ⲞⲨⲬⲒⲬ Ⲉ[ⲤⲬⲀⲢ ⲌⲈ]Ⲛ Ⲟ[ⲨⲘⲈⲦ]ⲀⲦⲚⲈⲒ: the translator interpreted the LXX as ἀνελεημόνως χειρὶ κραταιᾷ *sine commate*. In the Bohairic and Sahidic versions, ἀνελεημόνως is taken as belonging to the first clause, χειρὶ κραταιᾷ with the second. Note also the transposition of the two phrases in the Michigan papyrus.
　　2 ⲬⲒⲬ: Bohairic; ⲬⲒⲬⲌ Fayumic, but cf. ⲬⲈⲨⲬ as plural in Fay.[1]

---

[1] Unless otherwise noted, all information about dialect forms is taken from Crum, *Dict.*

3 [ⲬⲀⲢ: Fay.; ⲬⲞⲢ, Boh., is also possible.

ⲘⲈⲦ]: ⲘⲈⲦ- BF; ⲘⲚⲦ-, found in P. Mich. inv. 3521 (Husselman, *Gospel of John*; e.g. 9.8) and Oxyrhynchite (*P. Mil. Copti*; e.g. 22r25; cf. Kasser, *Compléments morphol.*), is also possible.

6 Note that the Michigan papyrus omits from the translation καὶ ἀπέρριψάς με ἀπὸ σωτηρίας. The phrase is translated in the Bohairic and Sahidic versions. For its omission in other versions, see Rahlfs' apparatus *ad loc.*

ⲈⲒ]ⲘⲒ: (Ⲉ)ⲒⲘⲒ F; the space appears to be too ample for ⲒⲘⲒ. The alternation of initial ⲈⲒ and Ⲓ is also found in Oxyrhynchite: Quecke, *P. Mil. Copti* 96. Similarly, ⲈⲒ]ⲠⲒ in line 11 suits the space better than does ⲒⲠⲒ.

6f Ⲛ[ⲬⲈ: here and in V 3 Ⲛ[ⲬⲒ is also possible. Note that P. Mich. inv. 3521 has ⲚⲬⲒ while 3520 has ⲚⲬⲈ (Husselman, *Gospel of John* 43 n. 18). ⲚϬⲎ, Ox. (*P. Mil. Copti*; Kasser, *Compléments morphol.*), seems too large. On the various spellings of ⲚϬⲒ, see Kahle, *Bala'izah* I 266 n. 1.

10 ⲌⲀⲦⲂ]Ⲉ[Ⲧ] Ⲏ: Ⲏ, though doubtful, seems better than ⲒⲈ (B); cf. the Ⲏ in ⲈⲌⲢⲎⲒ, V 7. Ⲏ appears in P. Mich. inv. 3521 (John 9.21). Although paleographically less likely, the reading -ⲈⲚ ⲠⲘⲞ]Ⲩ [Ⲛ]ⲈⲒ (cf. Sahidic version, apparatus), cannot be excluded.

11 ⲚϤⲈⲒ]ⲠⲒ etc.: the reading and restoration are conjectural; neither the Bohairic nor the Sahidic version offers a close parallel. For the phraseology, cf. the following passages in Sahidic: Gen. 18.6 (Ciasca) ⲀⲢⲒⲢⲈ ⲚⲦⲈⲒⲌⲈ, 1 Kgs. 11.7 (Drescher) ⲈⲨⲈⲈⲒⲢⲈ ⲚⲦⲈⲒⲌⲈ ⲌⲰϢϤ ⲚⲚⲈϤⲈⲞⲞⲨ. Instead of ⲚⲈⲒ, neither ⲚⲎⲒ nor ⲚⲀⲒ can be read. For ⲚⲈ=, a form common to F and Ox., see Quecke, *P. Mil. Copti* 90 and n. 27; Husselman, *Gospel of John* 13.

ⲌⲀⲒ/: probably ⲌⲀⲒ/[ⲠⲒⲘⲒ (cf. Boh. and Sah.).

V

1-3 In the first line the letter before ⲢⲈⲂ[is either Ⲉ or Ⲗ, and Ⲗ seems better. The appearance of ⲌⲈⲚⲌⲞⲞ[Ⲩ in 2, followed by Ⲍ]ⲈⲚⲌⲞⲞ[Ⲩ in 3, indicates that the translator is here paraphrasing the LXX (ἐγὼ δὲ ἐπέχων ἀγαθοῖς, ἰδοὺ συνήντησάν μοι μᾶλλον ἡμέραι κακῶν — see Rahlfs' app. for variants). The Sahidic version[2] suggests Ⲅ]ⲀⲢ at the beginning of line 1, but I am then unable to offer any convincing restoration for what follows. Perhaps, instead of Ⲅ]ⲀⲢ, ⲌⲦ]ⲀⲢ (i.e. ⲌⲦⲞⲢ) should be restored: if so, the text may have run as follows: ... ⲌⲈⲚ ⲌⲈⲚ/[ⲌⲦ]ⲀⲢ ⲈⲂ[ⲞⲖ ⲬⲈ ⲌⲀⲒ-ϢⲰⲠⲒ ⲌⲈ]/Ⲛ ⲌⲈⲚⲌⲞⲞ[Ⲩ ⲈⲚⲀⲚⲞⲨⲞⲨ ⲌⲈⲒⲦⲈ (Fay.) (Ⲍ)]/ⲀⲨⲦⲀⲌⲞⲒ, etc., "... in constraints [i.e. ἐν ἀνάγκαις, 25], because I lived in good days: behold evil days befell me..."

---

[2] Ciasca prints ⲈⲒϢⲞⲞⲠ ⲌⲰ ⲌⲚ ⲚⲀⲀⲄⲀⲐⲞⲚ, but he seems to have confused his principal manuscript (as reported by E. Amélineau, "The Sahidic Translation of the Book of Job," *TSBA* 9 [1893] 456: ⲈⲒϢⲞⲞⲠ ⲄⲀⲢ ⲌⲚ ⲚⲀⲀⲄⲀⲐⲞⲚ) with the variant reading in the apparatus: ⲈⲒϢⲞⲞⲠ ⲌⲰ ⲌⲚ ⲌⲈⲚⲀⲄⲀⲐⲞⲚ.

With this restoration, μᾶλλον remains untranslated, as it does in one of the Sahidic witnesses (see the app. to the Sah. version).

3f ЄУ2Ѧ]/ОУ: the space appears to be too short for a reading modeled upon either the Bohairic (ΝΤЄ 2ѦΝΠЄΤ2ШОУ) or the Sahidic (ΜΠЄΘΟΟУ).

4 Note that verse 27 is omitted in this version, as well as in the Boh. and Sah.; cf. CIASCA, *Fragm. copto-sahid.* II p. XXVIII.

ОУ[ѦШ: or ОУ[ЧI, the Bohairic idiom (CRUM, *Dict.* 24b).

5 2ѦIΟУ[Ш2: though not certain, У looks better than anything else; paleographically unattractive, 2ѦIΟ2[I ЄРѦТ (cf. Boh.) is also too long for the space. If -ОУ[Ш2 is right, it is used in the sense of "to be placed, lie, dwell." Cf. e.g. Acts 2.26 (Thompson, Horner) ΤѦΚЄСѦРΞ ΝѦОУШ2 2Ν ОУ2ЄѦΠIС.

6 СУΝѦΓШΓΗ: here renders ἐκκλησία; for the tendency on the part of Coptic translators to use one Greek word to render another, see e.g. DRESCHER, *Kingdoms I, II* Textus p. 192, Versio p. VI.

7f [ЄΝIСΗ]/ΦΗΝОС: ЄΝIСIΦΗΝОС, more suited to the available space, may have been written.

9 ΝѦΚЄ[С: though the space permits, ΝѦΚЄ[ЄС is less likely in view of the preceding ΠѦШЄР. Note also the occurrence of ΝѦΚЄС in a fragment from an early Coptic manuscript of Job, published by CRUM, *WS*: p. 30 Verso, line 1. On the dialect of this text, which has some similarities with the Michigan piece, see KAHLE, *Bala'izah* I 220ff.

10 ХШХI: in Sahidic, ХШ(Ш)6Є (CRUM, *Dict.* 800b). I cannot parallel this as a form of ХШ(Ш)6Є, but it is comparable to Bohairic ХШХI (= Sah. 6ШШХЄ; CRUM, *Dict.* 841a).

ЄВОѦ: О is damaged but certain, and ЄВѦѦ cannot be read.

3

I CORINTHIANS 4.9-5.3

P. Mich. inv. 4951　　　　15.2 × 36.6 cm.　　　　9th cent.

This piece is described in Worrell, *Mich.* p. 10; the outer column of a leaf from a large vellum codex, it provides a continuous text of I Cor. 4.9-5.3. The page number $\overline{\Lambda Є}$ appears in the upper right corner of the recto, which also contains the title [ΤЄΠРОС ΚОРIΝΘ]IОУС Ѧ̄, and the upper left corner of the verso is marked $\overline{\Lambda \text{S}}$. The piece should probably be assigned to the ninth century: cf. e.g. Stegemann, *Paläographie* Pl. 15 (Morgan 577: A.D. 896).

Below the transcription, I provide a collation with the editions of
Horner and Thompson. The only new reading of significance is in
V i 3-5 (I Cor. 4.17), which is closer to the word order of the Greek
than are the other Sahidic texts (see note ad loc.). For a description
of the method employed in collation, see above, p. XV.

Recto (Hair Side)
Col. ii

[ΤΕΠΡΟΣ ΚΟΡΙΝΘ]ΙΟΥС Ᾱ	ΛΕ	
ΑΡΗΥ ΓΑΡ ΝΤΑ ΠΝΟΥΤΕ		4.9
ΚΑΑΝ ΝΑΠΟСΤΟΛΟС Ν		
ΖΑΕ· ΝΘΕ ΝΝΙΕΠΙΘΑΝΑ		
ΤΗС· ΧΕ ΑΝΨΩΠΕ Ν̇		
5	ΘΕΑΔΡΟΝ Μ̇ΠΚΟСΜΟС·	
[Α]ΥΩ ΝΑΓΓΕΛΟС ΜΝ̇ Ν̇		
ΡΩΜΕ· ΑΝΟΝ ΑΝΕΡ СΟϬ		10
ΕΤΒΕ ΠΕΧ̄С̄· Ν̇ΤΩΤΝ̇		
ΔΕ Ν̇ΤΕΤΝ̇ ΖΝ̇СΑΒΕ· ΖΜ		
10	ΠΕΧ̄С̄· ΑΝΟΝ ΤΕΝ̇ϬΟΟΒ·	
Ν̇ΤΩΤΝ̇ ΔΕ ΤΕΤΝΧΟ		
ΟΡ· Ν̇ΤΩΤΝ ΤΕΤΝ̄		
ΤΑΕΙΗΥ· ΑΝΟΝ ΔΕ ΤΝ̄		
СΝΨ· ΨΑ ΖΡΑΪ Ε†ΟΥ		11
15	ΝΟΥ· ΤΝ̄ΝΕΖΚΟΕΙΤ·	
ΤΝΟΒΕ· ΤΝ̄ΚΗΚ ΑΖΗΥ·		
СΕ† ΚΛ̄Ψ ΕΧΩΝ· ΤΝ̄		
ΨΤΕΡΤΩΡ· ΤΝ̇ΖΟСΕ·		12
[Ε]ΝΕΡ ΖΩΒ ΕΝΕΝ̇ϬΙΧ Μ̇		

20   ΜΙΝ ΜΜΟΝ· ΕΥСΑϨΟΥ

ΜΜΟΝ· ΤΝ̇СΜΟΥ ΕΡΟΟΥ·

ΕΥΠΗΤ Ν̇СѠΝ· ΤΝ̇Α

ΝΕΧΕ   ΜΜΟΟΥ· ΕΥϪΙ   13

ΟΥΑ ΕΡΟΝ· ΤΝ̇ΠΑΡΑΚΑ

25   ΛΕΙ Μ̇ΜΟΟΥ· Ν̇ΘΕ ΝΝΙ

ΠΕΡΙΚΑΘΑΡΜΑ ΜΠΚΟС

[Μ]ΟС· ΑΝΕΡ ѰΒΕ ΝΟΥΟΝ

[ΝΙ]Μ· ѰΑ ϨΡΑΪ ΕϮΟΥΝΟΥ·

[Ν]ΝΕΙϮ ѰΙΠΕ ΝΗΤΝ̅ ΑΝ   14

30   [ΕΙСϨ]ΑΪ ΝΗΤΝ̅ Ν̇ΝΑΪ·

[ΑΛ]Λ̣Α ΕΪϮ СΒѠ ΝΗΤΝ̅

[ϨѠ]С ѰΗΡΕ ΜΜΕΡΙΤ·

[ΚΑΝ Ε]ѰѠΠΕ ΟΥΝΤΗ   15

[ΤΝ] ΜΜΑΥ ΝΟΥΤΒΑ

35   [ΜΠΑ]ΙΔΑΓΟΓΟС ϨΜ ΠΕ

[Χ̅С̅] ΑΛΛΑ Ν̇ϨΑϨ ΝΕΙѠΤ

[Α]Ν ΑΝΟΚ ΓΑΡ ΑΪϪΠΕ

[ΤΗΥ]ΤΝ̅ ϨΜ ΠΕΧ̅С̅ Ι̅С̅

[ϨΙΤΜ] ΠΕΥΑΓΓΕΛΙΟΝ

Verso (Flesh Side)

Col. i

Λ̅Ϩ̅

ϮΠΑΡΑΚΑΛΕΙ ϬΕ Μ̅ΜѠ   16

ΤΝ ΤΕΝΤΝ̅ ΤΗ[Υ]

ΤΝ ΕΡΟΪ· ΕΤΒΕ ΠΑΙ Α[Ι]   17

TNNOOY NHTN N̄T[I]

5   MOΘEOC· ETE ΠAI ΠE [ΠA]

ϢHPE M̄MEPIT· AY[Ϣ]

MΠICTOC 2M ΠⲬOEI[C]

ΠAI ETNATPETETN̄

P̄ ⲠMEEYE NNA2IOOYE

10   ET2M ΠEⲬⲤ· NΘE E††

CBϢ MMOC 2N NEKK

ΛHCIA THPOY 2M̄ MA

NIM· 2ⲰC N†NHY   18

AN ϢAPⲰTN̄· A2OINE

15   ⲬICE N̄2HT· †NHY ΔE   19

ϢAPⲰTN̄ 2N OYGEΠH

EPϢAN ΠⲬOEIC P 2NA[Ϥ]

NTAEIME AN EΠϢA[ⲬE]

N̄NETⲬOCE N̄2HT·

20   AΛΛA TEYGOM· TM[NTE]   20

PO ΓAP M̄ΠNOYTE NEC

2N̄ 2N̄ϢAⲬE AN· AΛ[ΛA]

2N OYGOM· OY ΠETE   21

TNOYAϢϤ̄ TAEI ϢA

25   PⲰTN̄ 2N OYGEPⲰϤ

ⲬE 2N OYAΓAΠH· M[N]

OYΠN̄A M̄MN̄T̄PM̄[PAϢ]

CECⲰTM PⲰ EYΠOPN[IA]   5.1

N̄2HT THYTN̄) E[NC]

ⲀⲨⲰ ⲞⲨⲠⲞⲢⲚⲒⲀ ⲚⲦⲈⲒⲘⲒⲚⲈ

30   ⲌⲚ ⲚⲔⲈⲌⲈⲐⲚⲞⲤ Ⲁ[Ⲛ]

       ⲌⲰⲤⲦⲈ ⲈⲦⲢⲈ ⲞⲨⲀ Ⲝ[Ⲓ ⲐⲒⲘⲈ]

       ⲘⲠⲈⳞⲈⲒⲰⲦ· Ⲁ[ⲨⲰ Ⲛ]   2

       ⲦⲰⲦⲚ ⲦⲈⲦⲚⲜ[ⲞⲤⲈ Ⲛ]

       ⲌⲎⲦ· ⲀⲨⲰ ⲚⲦⲀ[ⲦⲈⲦⲚⲢ]

35   ⲌⲎⲂⲈ ⲀⲚ ⲚⲌⲞⲨⲞ Ⲝ[ⲈⲔⲀⲤ]

       ⲈⳞⲈⳞⲈⲒ ⲌⲚ ⲦⲈⲦⲚ[ⲘⲎⲦⲈ]

       ⲘⲠⲚⲦⲀⳞⲈⲒⲢⲈ [ⲘⲠⲈⲒ]

       ⲌⲰⲂ· ⲀⲚⲞⲔ ⲄⲀ[Ⲣ ⲈⲚ⳦]   3

       ⲌⲀⲦⲈ ⲐⲎⲨⲦⲚ Ⲁ[Ⲛ ⲌⲘ]

40   ⲠⲤⲰⲘⲀ· ⲈⲒⲌ[ⲀⲦⲈ]

       ⲐⲎⲨⲦⲚ ⲆⲈ Ⲍ[Ⲙ ⲠⲈⲠⲚⲀ]

Collation with H(orner) and Th(ompson)

4.9 ⲚⲀⲄⲄⲈⲖⲞⲤ H*app* Th*app*: ⲚⲚⲀⲄⲄⲈⲖⲞⲤ HTh   10 ⲚⲦⲰⲦⲚ³ H*app* Th: ⲚⲦⲰⲦⲚ ⲆⲈ H   11 ⲦⲚⲚⲈⲌⲔⲞⲈⲒⲦ: ⲦⲚⲌⲔⲀⲈⲒⲦ HTh   12 ⲈⲚⲈⲚⳞⲒⲜ: ⲌⲚ ⲚⲈⲚⳞⲒⲜ HTh 17 Ⲁ[Ⲓ]ⲦⲚⲚⲞⲞⲨ ⲚⲎⲦⲚ ⲚⲦ[Ⲓ]ⲘⲞⲐⲈⲞⲤ: ⲀⲒⲦⲚⲚⲞⲞⲨ ⲚⲦⲒⲘⲞⲐⲈⲞⲤ ⲚⲎⲦⲚ H, ⲀⲒⲦⲚⲚⲈⲨ ⲦⲒⲘⲞⲐⲈⲞⲤ ⲚⲎⲦⲚ Th   ⲈⲦⲚⲀⲦⲢⲈⲦⲈⲚ-: ⲈⲦⲚⲀⲦⲢⲈⲚ- HTh   18 ⳦ⲚⲎⲨ Th*app*: ⳦ⲚⲎⲨ ⲆⲈ HTh   20 ⲚⲈⲤⲌⲚ ⲌⲚⳛⲀⲬⲈ Th*app* (ⲚⲈⲤⲌⲈⲚ ⲌⲚⳛ.): ⲚⲈⲤⳛⲚ ⳛ. H(ⲚⲚⲈⲤ-)Th   21 ⲬⲈ: ⲬⲚ HTh 5.2 ⲠⲚⲦⲀⳞⲈⲒⲢⲈ ⲘⲠⲈⲒⲌⲰⲂ Th (ⲠⲈⲚⲦⲀⳞ-, ⲠⲈⲈⲒ-): ⲠⲈⲚⲦⲀⳞⲢ ⲠⲈⲒⲌⲰⲂ H

R ii

Tit.: the restoration is modeled on the subscription in Thompson's edition, ⲦⲈⲠⲢⲞⲤ :ⲔⲞⲢⲒⲚⲐⲒⲞⲨⲤ Ⲁ̄:

15 -ⲔⲞⲈⲒⲦ: i.e. -ⲔⲀⲈⲒⲦ (see Crum, *Dict.* 663b).

19 [Ⲉ]ⲚⲈⲢ ⲌⲰⲂ ⲈⲚⲈⲚⳞⲒⲜ: literally, "as we work *at* our hands." The correct text, with ⲌⲚ ⲚⲈⲚⳞⲒⲜ, is given in Horner and Thompson: "as we work *with* our hands" (ἐργαζόμενοι ταῖς ἰδίαις χερσίν). The reading in the Michigan text may have arisen as follows: 1) ⲌⲚ → Ⲛ; for the pervasive omission of hori, see e.g. Kahle, *Bala'izah* I 139-142; 2) Ⲛ → Ⲉ; *ibid.* 114f. See also No. 10 in this volume, note to V 8.

V i

3-5 **Λ[Ι]ΤΝΝΟΟΥ ΝΗΤΝ ΝΤ[Ι]ΜΟΘΕΟC**: this reproduces the Greek word order with accuracy: ἔπεμψα ὑμῖν Τιμόθεον. In the other Sahidic witnesses, **ΝΗΤΝ** follows **ΤΙΜΟΘΕΟC** (see Collation). (Note also the word order in the Bohairic: **ΛΙΟΥШΡΠ ΝШΤΕΝ ΝΤΙΜΟΘΕΟC**, Horner.)

22 **2Ν 2ΝШΑΧΕ**: the original had **2Ν ШΑΧΕ** (see Collation, and cf. the Greek, which has the singular noun: ἐν λόγῳ). The mistake arose through dittography, and the second **2Ν** was interpreted as the indefinite article, on analogy with **2Ν ΟΥ6ΟΜ** immediately following.

26 **ΧΕ**: i.e. **ΧΝ** (see Collation and CRUM, *Dict.* 772a).

29f The interlinear addition and the curved insertion mark after **ΤΗΥΤΝ** seem to be in a second hand.

4

I CORINTHIANS 11.10-28

P. Mich. inv. 4563   Fragment 1: 8.8 × 9.7 cm.   6th or 7th cent.
　　　　　　　　　　 Fragment 2: 10.2 × 9.3 cm.

Catalogued in Worrell, *Mich.* p. 10, the present text consists of two fragments from a single folio of a papyrus codex. Parts of the left and right margins remain, but both pieces are broken off at the top and bottom. The following table shows the portion of text preserved in the Michigan papyrus:

Fragment 1 Recto: I Cor. 11.10-12
Fragment 2 Recto: I Cor. 11.16-18
Fragment 2 Verso: I Cor. 11.22-23
Fragment 1 Verso: I Cor. 11.26-28

Though not contiguous, the two fragments clearly come from the same portion of the leaf. This is shown by the contour of the pieces: the sheet was folded vertically, then broken, and the damaged area in the margin of the first fragment mirrors that in the margin of the second. Note also that, from a comparison of the text in Horner and Thompson, we can calculate that an average of 20 lines is lost between Fr. 1 R and Fr. 2 R, between Fr. 2 R and Fr. 2 V, and between Fr. 2 V and Fr. 1 V. Since the same amount of material is missing between the fragments, it follows that they occupied the same relative position on the sheet. We are dealing with a bicolumnar codex, with Fragment 1 comprising Col. i R and Col. ii V, and Fragment 2 Col. ii R and Col. i V.

On the basis of the hand, the text should probably be assigned to the sixth or seventh century. Though considerably less graceful, it bears a certain resemblance to Cramer, *Paläographie* No. 16 (6th/7th).

I have collated the text with the editions of Horner and Thompson. The only new reading is in R ii 6f (11.18), where the papyrus reads ⲉⲧ[ⲉⲧⲛϣ]ⲁⲛⲥⲱⲟⲩⲍ, against ⲉⲧⲉⲧⲛⲥⲱⲟⲩⲍ in Horner and Thompson. Here the Greek has συνερχομένων ὑμῶν, which the circumstantial ⲉⲧⲉⲧⲛⲥⲱⲟⲩⲍ renders literally. The conditional in the Michigan text should be taken in a temporal sense: "whenever you assemble."

RECTO

Col. i		Col. ii	
↑ [ⲃⲉ ⲛⲁ]ⲅⲅⲉⲗⲟ[ⲥ ⲡⲗⲏⲛ]	11.10, 11	[ⲛⲟⲩ]ⲧⲉ· [ⲡⲁⲓ ⲇⲉ ϯⲡⲁ]	11.16, 17
[ⲙⲛ ⲥ]ⲋⲓⲙⲉ ⲁ̄[ϫⲛ ⲍⲟ]		[ⲣⲁⲅ]ⲅⲓⲗⲉ ⲙⲙ[ⲟϥ ⲉⲓ]	
[ⲟⲩ]ⲧ ⲟⲩⲇ[ⲉ ⲍⲟⲟⲩⲧ]		[ⲁⲓⲡⲉ]ⲛⲟⲩ ⲁⲛ [ϫⲉ ⲉ]	
[ⲛⲟ]ⲩⲉϣ ⲛ̄ⲥ[ⲋⲓⲙⲉ ⲍⲙ]		[ⲧⲉⲧⲛ]ⲥⲱⲟⲩⲍ [ⲁⲛ ⲉⲩ]	
5 ⲡϫⲟⲉⲓⲥ· ⲛ[ⲑⲉ ⲅⲁⲣ]	12	[ϫⲓⲥ]ⲉ ⲁⲗⲗⲁ ⲉⲩⲍⲏⲃ[ⲉ]	
ⲛ̄ⲧⲉⲥⲋⲓⲙⲉ [ⲉⲟⲩⲉⲃⲟⲗ]		[ϣⲟ]ⲣⲡ̄ ⲙⲉⲛ ⲅⲁⲣ ⲉⲧ̄[ⲉ]	18
ⲍⲙ̄ ⲡⲍⲟⲟⲩⲧ [ⲧⲉ]		[ⲧⲛϣ]ⲁⲛⲥⲱⲟⲩⲍ ⲉ̄ⲍⲟⲩⲛ	
ⲧⲁⲓ̈ ⲧⲉ ⲑⲉ ⲙ[ⲡⲍⲟⲟⲩⲧ ⲉ]		[ⲍⲛ] ⲧⲉⲕⲕⲗⲏⲥⲓⲁ· ϯ	
ⲟⲩⲉ̄ⲃⲟⲗ ⲍⲛ̄ [ⲧⲉⲥⲋⲓ]		[ⲥⲱ]ⲧⲙ̄ ϫⲉ ⲟⲩⲛ ⲍⲛ̄ⲡϣ	
10 ⲙⲉ ⲡⲉ : ⲡⲧ[ⲏⲣϥ ⲇⲉ]		[ⲡϫ] ⲛ̄ⲍⲏⲧ ⲑⲩⲧⲛ̄·	
[ⲍⲛⲉⲃ]ⲟ̣ⲗ ⲋ̣[ⲙ ⲡⲛⲟⲩⲧⲉ]		[ⲁⲩ]ⲱ ϯⲡ̄ⲓⲥⲧⲉⲩⲉ̄ ⲍⲛ̄	
(Ca. 20 lines missing)		(Ca. 20 lines missing)	

VERSO

Col. i   Col. ii

→ [ΑΥШ ΕΤ]ΕΤⲚ̄ϯ [ШΙΠΕ]   11.22   [ΤΑ]ШΕ ΟΕ[ΙШ ΜΠ]   11.26

  [ΝΝΕΤ]Ε ΜⲚ̄Τ[ΑΥ]   [ΜΟΥ Μ]ΠΧΟΕ[ΙC ШΑΝ]

  [ΤΑΧΟΟ]C ΝΗΤ[Ν ΧΕ ΟΥ]   [ΤϤΕΙ] ϨШCΤ[Ε ΠΕΤΝΑ]   27

  [ΤΑ]ΑΙΠΕΝΟΥ Μ̄[ΜШΤΝ]   [ΟΥШ]Μ Μ̄ΠΟΕ[ΙΚ]

5 [Ϩ]Μ ΠΑΪ· Ⲛ̄ϯΑΙ[ΠΕ]   [ΝϤCШ Μ̄ΠΑΠ[ΟΤ ΜΠ]

  ΝΟΥ ΑΝ : ΑΝ[ΟΚ]   23   [ΧΟΕΙC] ΕΝϤΜ̄ΠШΑ

  ΓΑΡ ΑΪΧΙ ΕΒΟΛ ϨΪ[ΤΜ]   [ΑΝ Ϥ]ΝΑШΠΕ Ⲛ̄

  ΠΧΟΕΪC Μ̄ΠΕ[ΝΤΑΙ]   [ΕΝΟ]ΧΟC Μ̄ΠCШΜΑ

  ΤΑΑϤ ΝΗΤⲚ̄· Χ[Ε ΠΧΟ]   [ΜΝ ΠΕC]ΝΟϤ Μ̄ΠΧΟΕΙC —

10 ΕΪC ῙC̄ ϨⲚ̄ ΤΕΥШ[Η]   [ΜΑΡΕ] ΠΡШΜΕ ΔΕ ΔΟ   28

                               [ΚΙΜΑΖ]Ε Μ̄Μ[Ο]Ϥ· ΑΥШ

  (Ca. 20 lines missing)

  ——— — — —

Collation with H(orner) and Th(ompson) (See above, p. XV) 11.12 Ϩ[Μ : see commentary   17 ϨΗΒΕ Th*app*: ϨΒΒΕ HTh   18 ΕΤΕΤΝШΑΝCШΟΥϨ: ΕΤΕΤΝCШΟΥϨ HTh
ϯΠΙCΤΕΥΕ ϨΝ H*app*Th: ϯΠΙCΤΕΥΕ Ν H   27 Μ̄ΠCШΜΑ HTh*app*: ΕΠCШΜΑ Th

R i

    1 I.e. ΕΤ]/[ΒΕ.
    6 [ΕΟΥΕΒΟΛ]: the restoration is modeled on Horner (Thompson has the or-
thographic variant ΕΥΕΒΟΛ); see also 8f.
    11 [ϨΝ: the space does not permit ϨΕΝ; for ϨΝ see below, R ii 9.
    Ϩ[Μ ΠΝΟΥΤΕ: so Thompson; also possible is Ϩ[ΙΤΜ ΠΝΟΥ/ΤΕ (Horner).

R ii

    3 [ΑΙΠΕ]ΝΟΥ: for the spelling, see V i 4f.

5

II CORINTHIANS 12.21-13.12

P. Mich. inv. 552   16.2 × 20.5 cm.   9th cent.

This text is thus described in Worrell, *Mich.* p. 11: "Two fragments making up the larger part of a parchment folio numbered PNΘ-PΞ. The inner corners of the leaf are broken off and about three lines at the bottom are lost." On the basis of the hand, the piece should be assigned to the ninth century: it is quite similar to Cramer, *Paläographie* No. 23 (A.D. 890).

Below the text I provide a collation with the editions of Horner and Thompson.

Recto (Hair Side)

$$\overline{\text{PN}\Theta}$$

	[ΜΝ ΠⳬⲰⲰϥ ⲈΝΤ]ⲀⲨⲀ̄Ⲁϥ · —	12.21
	[ΠΜⲈⲌ ⲮⲞΜΝ]Τ̄ Ν̄ⲤⲞΠ ΠⲈ ΠⲀⲒ̈	13.1
	[†ΝΗⲨ ⲮⲀΡ]ⲰΤΝ̄ ⲌⲒ̈ΤΝ̄ Τ̄ΤⲀΠ	
	[ΡⲞ ΜΜ]Ν̄ΤΡⲈ Ⲥ̄ΝⲀⲨ Η̄ ⲮⲞΜΝ̄Τ	
5	[ⲈΡⲈ Ⲯ]ⲀϪⲈ ΝⲒ̈Μ Ⲁ̄ⲌⲈΡⲀΤϥ·	
	[ⲀⲒ̈ϪⲞⲞ]Ⲥ ⲄⲀΡ ϪⲒ̈Ν Ν̄ⲮⲞΡΠ̄ ⲀⲨⲰ	2
	[ⲞΝ †Ⲯ ΡΠ] ϪⲰ Μ̄ΜⲞⲤ	
	[ⲌⲰⲤ ⲈⲒ̈]ⲌⲀΤΝ̄ ΤΗⲨΤΝ̄ Μ̄⟨Π⟩ΜⲈⲌ Ⲥ̄Η̄ Ⲥ̄	
	[ΝⲀⲨ] ⲀⲨⲰ ⲞΝ ⲈΝ†ⲌⲀΤΝ̄ ΤΗⲨ	
10	[ΤΝ Ⲁ]Ν ΤⲈΝⲞⲨ· ⲈⲒ̈ⲤⲌⲀⲒ̈ Ν̄ΝⲈΝΤⲀⲨⲢ̄	
	[ΝⲞΒ]Ⲉ ϪⲒ̈Ν Ν̄ⲮⲞΡΠ̄ ⲀⲨⲰ Μ̄ΠⲔ[ⲈⲤ]ⲈⲈ̄	
	ΠⲈ ΤΗΡϥ·	
	[Ϫ Ⲉ] ⲈⲒ̈ⲮⲀΝⲈⲒ̈ Ν̄ⲔⲈⲤⲞΠ Ν̄†ΝⲀ† [Ⲥ]Ⲟ	
	[Ⲁ]Ν· Ⲉ̄ΒⲞⲖ ϪⲈ Ⲉ̄ΤⲈΤΝ̄ⲮⲒ̈ΝⲈ Ν̄ⲤⲀ Τ	3

15 [Δ]ΟΚΙΜΗ ⲘⲠⲈⲬⲤ ⲈⲦⲰⲀϪⲈ ⲚⲌⲎⲦ

   [ⲠⲀⲒ Ⲉ]ⲦⲈ ⲚϤⲞ ⲀⲚ ⲚⲀⲦϬⲞⲘ ⲈⲌⲞⲨⲚ

   [ⲈⲢⲰ]ⲦⲚ· ⲀⲖⲖⲀ ϤϬⲘ ϬⲞⲘ ⲚⲌⲎⲦ

   [ⲐⲨⲦ]Ⲛ· ⲔⲀⲒ ⲄⲀⲢ ⲚⲦⲀⲨⲤ̄ϤⲞⲨ   4

   [ⲘⲘⲞϤ ⲈⲂ]ⲞⲖ ⲌⲚ ⲞⲨⲀⲤⲐⲈⲚⲒⲀ·

20 [ⲀⲖⲖⲀ ϤⲞⲚⲌ Ⲉ̄]ⲂⲞⲖ ⲌⲚ ⲦϬⲞⲘ ⲘⲠⲚⲞⲨ

   [ⲦⲈ ⲔⲀⲒ ⲄⲀⲢ ⲀⲚ]ⲞⲚ ⲌⲰⲰⲚ ⲦⲚϬⲞ

   [ⲞⲂ ⲚⲌⲎⲦϤ ⲀⲖⲖⲀ] ⲦⲚⲚⲀⲰ̄ⲚⲌ̄

   [ⲚⲘⲘⲀϤ ⲈⲂⲞⲖ ⲌⲚ ⲦϬⲞ]Ⲙ ⲘⲚ̄ⲚⲞⲨⲦⲈ

   [ⲈⲌⲞⲨⲚ ⲈⲢⲰⲦⲚ   ]

25 [ϪⲚⲦ ⲐⲨⲦⲚ ϪⲈ ⲦⲈⲦⲚⲌⲚ ⲦⲠⲒⲤ]ⲦⲒ̄Ⲥ   5

———————————————

(ca. 3 lines missing)

Verso (Flesh Side)

Ⲣ̄Ⲝ̄

ⲚⲦⲈⲦⲚ̄ ⲌⲚ̄Ϫ[ⲞⲞⲨⲦ ⲦⲚⲀⲌⲦⲈ ⲆⲈ ϪⲈ ⲦⲈ]   13.5, 6

ⲦⲚ̄ⲚⲀⲈⲒⲘⲈ ϪⲈ Ⲁ[ⲚⲞⲚ ⲀⲚ ⲌⲈⲚϪⲞⲞⲨⲦ ⲀⲚ]

ⲦⲚ̄ⲰⲖⲎⲖ ⲆⲈ ⲈⲠⲚ[ⲞⲨⲦⲈ ⲈⲦⲘⲦⲢⲈ(ⲦⲈ)]   7

ⲦⲚ̄Ⲣ̄ ⲖⲀⲀⲨ ⲘⲠⲈⲐⲞⲞ[Ⲩ ϪⲈⲔⲀⲤ ⲀⲚ]

5   ⲀⲚⲞⲚ ⲈⲚⲚⲀⲞⲨⲰ̄Ⲛ[Ⲍ ⲈⲂⲞⲖ ⲚⲤⲰⲦⲠ]

   ⲀⲖⲖⲀ ϪⲈⲔⲀⲤ Ⲛ̄ⲦⲰⲦ[Ⲛ ⲈⲦⲈⲦⲚⲈⲢ]

      Ⲡ̄ⲠⲈⲦⲚ[Ⲁ]ⲚⲞⲨϤ·

   Ⲁ̄ⲚⲞⲚ ⲆⲈ ⲚⲦⲚⲰⲰⲠⲈ [ⲌⲰⲤ ⲤⲰⲦⲠ]

   ⲀⲚ· ⲘⲚ ϬⲞⲘ ⲄⲀⲢ· ⲘⲘⲞⲚ [Ⲉ̄Ⲧ ⲞⲨⲂⲈ Ⲧ]   8

10 ⲘⲈ· ⲀⲖⲖⲀ ⲈϪⲚ̄ ⲦⲘⲈ ⲦⲚ̄[ⲀⲢⲀⲰⲈ ⲄⲀⲢ]   9

ⲋⲟⲧⲁⲛ ⲁ̄ⲛⲟⲛ ⲉⲛⲩⲁⲛⲅⲃ̄ⲃ[ⲉ]

[ⲛ]ⲧⲱⲧⲛ̄ ⲁⲉ ⲛ̄ⲧⲉⲧⲛ̄ⲩⲱ[ⲡⲉ ⲉⲧ]

ⲉⲧⲛⲭⲟⲟⲣ· ⲡⲁⲓ̈ ⲣⲱ ⲡⲉⲧⲛ̄ⲩ[ⲗⲏⲗ]

ⲉ̄ⲣⲟϥ ⲉⲡⲉⲧⲛ̄ⲥⲟⲃⲧⲉ·

15   ⲉⲧⲃⲉ ⲡⲁⲓ̈ ⲉⲛⲧ̄ⲋⲁⲧⲛ̄ ⲑⲩⲧⲛ̄ [ⲁⲛ ⲧ]   10

ⲥ̄ⲋⲁⲓ̈ ⲛ̄ⲛⲁⲓ̈ ⲭⲉⲕⲁⲥ ⲛ̄ⲛⲁⲉⲓ̈ ⲧⲁⲭ[ⲣⲱ]

ⲋⲛ̄ ⲟⲩⲩⲱⲱⲧ ⲉ̄ⲃⲟⲗ ⲕⲁⲧ[ⲁ ⲧⲉ Ξ ⲟⲩ]

ⲥ̄ⲓ̄ⲁ̄ ⲛ̄ⲧⲁ ⲡ̄ⲭⲟⲉⲓ̈ⲥ ⲧⲁⲁⲥ ⲛⲁ[ⲓ ⲉⲩⲕⲱⲧ]

ⲁⲩ̄ⲱ̄ ⲉⲩⲩⲟⲣⲩ̄ⲣ ⲁⲛ· [

20   ⲧⲉⲛⲟⲩ ⲅⲉ ⲛⲁⲥⲛⲏⲩ ⲣⲁⲩ[ⲉ ⲥⲃⲧⲉ ⲑⲏⲩ]   11

ⲧⲛ̄ ⲥⲟⲡⲥ ⲙⲉⲉⲩⲉ ⲉⲡⲓ[ⲙⲉⲉⲩⲉ ⲛⲟⲩⲱⲧ]

ⲁⲣⲓ̈ ⲉⲓ̈ⲣⲏⲛⲏ· ⲁ[ⲩⲱ ⲡⲛⲟⲩⲧⲉ ⲛⲧ̄ⲣⲏ]

ⲛⲏ ⲙⲛ̄ ⲧⲁⲅ[ⲁⲡⲏ ⲛⲁⲩⲱⲡⲉ ⲛⲙ]

ⲙⲏⲧⲛ̄

25   ⲁⲥⲡⲁ[ⲍⲉ ⲛⲛⲉⲧⲛⲉⲣⲏⲩ ⲋⲛ ⲟⲩⲡⲓ ⲉⲥ]   12

ⲟⲩ[ⲁⲁⲃ

Collation with H(orner) and Th(ompson) (See above, p. XV)

13.1 ⲛⲥⲟⲡ HTh^{app}: om. Th   2 ⲋⲁⲧⲛ¹: ⲋⲁⲧⲉ HTh ⲋⲁⲧⲛ² Th: ⲋⲁⲧⲉ H
ⲙⲡⲕⲉⲥⲉⲉⲡⲉ HTh^{app}: ⲡⲕⲉⲥⲉⲉⲡⲉ Th   3 ⲉⲧⲉⲧⲛⲩⲓⲛⲉ Th^{app}: ⲧⲉⲧⲛ- HTh
5 ⲧⲉⲧⲛⲋⲛ Th: ⲉⲛⲧⲉⲧⲛ- H ⲋ(ⲉ)ⲛⲭⲟⲟⲩⲧ H^{app}Th: ⲋⲉⲛⲭⲟⲟⲩⲧ ⲁⲛ H   7 ⲧⲛ-
ⲱⲗⲏⲗ HTh^{app}: ⲧ- Th ⲉⲧⲙⲧⲣⲉⲧⲉⲧⲛ- H^{app}Th^{app}: ⲉⲧⲙⲧⲣⲉⲧⲛ- HTh ⲭⲉⲕⲁⲥ ⲁⲛ
ⲁⲛⲟⲛ ⲉⲛⲛⲁⲟⲩⲱⲛⲋ: ⲭ. ⲁⲛ ⲁⲛⲟⲛ ⲉⲛⲉ- HTh   9 ⲧⲛⲛⲁⲣⲁⲩⲉ H^{app}Th: ⲧⲛⲛⲁⲣⲁⲩⲉ ⲋⲱⲱⲛ H ⲉⲡⲉⲧⲛⲥⲟⲃⲧⲉ: ⲡⲉⲧⲛ- HTh   10 ⲋⲁⲧⲛ: ⲋⲁⲧⲉ HTh ⲧⲋⲋⲁⲓ
Th: ⲉⲓ- HTh^{app} 11 ⲥⲟⲡⲥ Th: ⲥⲟⲗⲥⲗ H

R

20 ⲉ̄]ⲃⲟⲗ: the supralinear stroke remains.

25 The space seems more suited to ⲧⲉⲧⲛ (Th) than to ⲉⲛⲧⲉⲧⲛ (H; i.e. ⲉⲛⲉ ⲧⲉⲧⲛ).

V

1 There does not appear to be enough room for ΛN (H) after ϨNX[OOYT.

3 ЄTMTPЄ(TЄ)-]: the space permits either the long or the short form of the second person plural.

10 There is no space for ϨⲰⲰN (H) after TNN[APAⲨЄ.

15 +]: (Th); also possible is ЄI] (HTh^{app}).

6

GALATIANS 5.11-6.1

P. Mich. inv. 3535a   3.2 × 8.3 cm.   4th or 5th cent.

This piece, composed of two contiguous fragments, is cited in Worrell, *Mich.* p. 8, where it is described as "the only Achmimic Biblical text" in the Michigan collection. Kahle mentions the text in *Bala'izah* I 273, in his list of early Coptic manuscripts, and he assigns it tentatively to the fourth or fifth century. Little remains to allow us to be precise about the dating, but the style is clearly early; its most noteworthy feature is ϭ made with the oblique stroke projecting from below: ⲇ (cf. J. Krall, "Über die Anfänge der koptischen Schrift," *MPER* 1 [1887] 111; Husselman, *Gospel of John* 42 n. 9; Stegemann, *Paläographie* 13).

Also indicative of an early date is the dialect. Because it admits ⲩ instead of ϩ in R 4 and probably in R 11 (see commentary), it is not pure Achmimic, and the text may belong to the group of manuscripts which are written in what Kahle calls "Achmimic with Subachmimic influence" (*Bala'izah* I 203). These texts belong to the fourth century, and this can be the date of the Michigan piece as well. Such a small amount survives, however, that it may be preferable to follow Kahle's approximate dating to the fourth or fifth century.

Recto and verso each preserve a narrow strip of writing (5-9 letters) which is eleven lines in length, with traces of a twelfth line. The papyrus seems to show the upper margin (0.8 cm.) on the verso; but the corresponding part of the recto is occupied with writing, and the original margin may now be lost. On the other three sides, the sheet is broken off.

The recto contains parts of Galatians 5.11-15, and the verso parts of 5.22-6.1. Comparison with the Sahidic and Bohairic versions shows deviations from both, but in general what remains resembles the Sahidic more often than it does the Bohairic. Only twice does the text agree with the Bohairic exclusively: R 2] . ⲰⲒⲀⲢⲀ: ... ⲚⲤⲰⲒ ⲌⲀⲢⲀ ... B, ... ⲘⲘⲞⲈⲒ ⲈⲒⲈ ... S; and V 7] .ⲎⲰⲞⲨⲈ[: ⲈⲎⲰⲞⲨⲒⲦ B, ⲚⲰⲞⲨⲰⲞ S). I have accordingly used the Sahidic as the basis for a purely exempli-gratia reconstruction, which I print below the diplomatic transcript. With the left and right margins missing, we can no longer determine the relative position of the Michigan papyrus on the original sheet, and consequently the line-by-line distribution of the reconstruction remains uncertain. I therefore use the format of a *texte suivi* and mark the surviving portions of the papyrus with suprascript line numbers. In the course of restoration I have found that only once does the Achmimic appear to offer a reading closer to the Bohairic than to the Sahidic (see below, on 5.23). For the reader's convenience I have added the pertinent sections from the Sahidic and Bohairic versions.

On the basis of the reconstruction, the number of letters on the recto varies from 20 to 29 per line, and on the verso, where the writing is more compressed, the range is from 29 to 36. If we posit an average line of 27 letters and assume that the amount of lost material from the end of R 12 to the beginning of V 1 was approximately the same as that in the Sahidic, then ca. 17-18 lines have been lost in the Michigan text. Since lines 1-12 on recto and verso are approximately 8.5 cm. in height, the missing lines would have occupied about 12.5 cm., and the original sheet, minus margins, would come to ca. 21 cm. Similarly, the original length of each line can be computed to be about 12 cm. To judge from its dimensions, the codex is most likely to have had a single column of writing per page. Its original format was probably similar to, though rather larger than, the Berlin codex of I Clement, which measures — excluding margins — 8 × 18 cm.; with its margins it extends to 12 × 25 cm. (see Schmidt, *Clemensbrief* 7f).[1]

---

[1] The codex of I Clement is included in Group 8 in TURNER, *Typology of the Codex* 431.

Recto (Margin?)		Verso (Margin)
→]ⲨⲘⲠⲤⲂⲂⲉ[	↑	]ⲄⲀⲠⲎⲠⲣⲉⲨⲉ[
] .ⲰⲒⲀⲣⲀⲀⲠⲉ[		]ⲬⲤ̄ⲧⲘⲚ̄ⲧⲠⲉ[
]ⲰⲤⲨⲉ. .ⲠⲰⲌ[		]ⲕⲣⲀⲧⲓⲀⲘⲚ̄Ⲛ[
]ⲉⲧⲨⲧⲀⲣⲧ[		]ⲚⲀⲠⲬ̄ⲤⲀⲉ[
5]ⲀⲨⲧⲀⲌⲘ. [	5	]Ⲛ̄ⲉⲠⲓⲑⲨⲘ[
] .ⲚⲎⲨⲘⲟ[		] .ⲌⲚⲉⲤⲉⲘ[
]ⲠⲉⲀⲨⲀ. [		] .ⲨⲨⲟⲨⲉ[
]ⲠⲎⲢ̄ⲄⲀ[		]ⲚⲓⲀⲚⲚ̄.[
] .ⲀⲣⲧⲎⲣ . [		] .ⲰⲰⲤⲌⲚ̄[
10]ⲀⲂⲀⲖⲌ[	10	]Ⲃ̄ⲧⲉⲠⲉⲓⲚ̄ⲧ[
] ⲉⲓⲧⲉⲨ[		]ⲘⲟⲨⲌⲀⲂⲀ[
] . [		] . .Ⲁ[

——— ———   ——— ———

(Ca. 17-18 lines missing)

R 2]ⲱ: corrected from Ⲩ?   ⲉ[: though damaged, ⲉ is certain
V 1]ⲅ: more likely than Ⲧ   3 Ⲛ̄[: Ⲙ also possible, but less likely   8 ⲓ: corrected from Ⲁ

Exempli-Gratia Reconstruction of Achmimic

R (5.11) ... ⲀⲓⲧⲀⲨⲉ Ⲁⲉⲓ[1]Ⲩ ⲘⲠⲤⲂⲂⲉ [ⲀⲌⲢⲀⲓ ⲀⲚ ⲤⲉⲢ ⲀⲓⲰⲕⲉ Ⲛ2]ⲤⲰⲓ
ⲀⲣⲀ ⲀⲠⲉ[ⲤⲕⲀⲚⲀⲀⲖⲟⲚ ⲘⲠ(ⲉ)ⲤⲢⲟⲤ ⲟⲨ3]ⲰⲤⲨ (12) ⲉ..ⲠⲰⲌ [ca. 15-20 4]
ⲉⲧⲨⲧⲀⲣⲧ[ⲣ(ⲉ) ⲘⲘⲰⲧⲚⲉ (13) ⲚⲧⲰⲧⲚⲉ ⲄⲀⲢ Ⲛ5]ⲀⲨⲧⲀⲌⲘ Ⲧ[ⲎⲚⲉ ⲀⲨⲘⲚⲧⲢⲘⲌⲉ
Ⲛ(ⲉ)6]ⲤⲚⲎⲨ Ⲙⲟ[ⲚⲟⲚ ⲧⲚⲘⲚⲧⲢⲘⲌⲉ ⲘⲚⲧⲤⲌⲰ7]Ⲡⲉ ⲀⲨⲀⲫ[ⲟⲢⲘⲎ ⲚⲧⲤⲀⲢⲌ ⲀⲖⲖⲀ ⲌⲓⲧⲚ
ⲧⲀⲄⲀ8]ⲠⲎ Ⲣ̄ ⲄⲀ[(ⲟ)ⲨⲀⲚ ⲚⲚⲉⲧⲚⲉⲢⲎⲨ (14) ⲠⲚⲟⲘⲟⲤ 9] ⲄⲀⲢ ⲧⲎⲢⲨ̄ [ⲌⲚ ⲟⲨⲨⲉⲬⲉ
ⲚⲟⲨⲰⲧ ⲚⲀⲨⲬⲰⲕ 10] ⲀⲂⲀⲖ Ⲍ[Ⲛ ⲀⲕⲀⲘⲢⲢⲉ ⲠⲉⲑⲓⲧⲟⲨⲰⲕ ⲚⲧⲕⲌⲉ 11] (15) ⲉⲓ ⲧⲉ
Ⲩ[ⲀⲧⲉⲧⲚ- ...

V (22) ... ΤΑ¹]ΓΑΠΗ ΠΡΕϢΕ [ϯΡΗΝΗ ΤΜΝΤϨΑΡϢ ϨΗΤ ΤΜΝΤ²]Χ̅C̅ ΤΜ̅Ν̅ΤΠΕ[ΤΝΑ-
ΝΟΥϤ ΤΠΙCΤΙC (23) ΤΜΝΤΡΜΡΕ(Ε)Ϥ ΤΕΓ³]ΚΡΑΤΙΑ ΜΝ̅ Ν̣[ΟΜΟC ϯ ΟΥΒΕ ΝΕΙ ΝΤΕΙ-
ΜΙΝΕ (24) ⁴] ΝΑ Π̅Χ̅C̅ ΔΕ [Ι̅C̅ ΑΥCⲣ̅ΟⲨ̅ ΝΤCΑΡΞ ΜΝ ΜΠΑΘΟC ΜΝ ⁵] Ν̅ΕΠΙΘΥΜ[Ι-
Α (25) ΕΙϨΠΕ ΤΝΑΝϨ ϨΜ Π(Ε)Π̅Ν̅Α̅ ± 5 ⁶].ϨΝΕCΕΜ[± 5 (26) ΜΝΤΝϨϢΠΕ ϨΝ
ΟΥΜΝΤΜΑΕΙ ΕΑΥ ⁷] ΕϤϢΟΥΕ[ΙΤ ΕΝΡ ΠΡΟΚΑΛΙ ΝΝΝΕΡΗΥ ΕΝΡ ΦΘΟ⁸]ΝΙ ΑΝΝΕ[ΡΗΥ
(6.1) Ν(Ε)CΝΗΥ ΕϨϢΠΕ ΑΝ ΑϢΑ ΟΥΡϢΜΕ (0-2) ⁹].ϢϢC ϨΝ [ΤΗΝΕ ΝΤϢΤΝΕ
Ν(Ε)ΠΝΕΥΜΑΤΙΚΟC C¹⁰]ΒΤΕ ΠΕΙ ΝΤ[ΕΙΜΙΝΕ ϨΝ ΟΥΠ̅Ν̅Α̅ ΜΜΝΤΡΜΡΕ(Ε)Ϥ ΕΚ¹¹-]
ΜΟΥϨ ΑΒΑ[Λ ΑΡΑΚ ϨΟΥΟΥΚ ΜΗΠϢC CΕΡ ΠΙΡΑϨΕ] ΜΜΑ[Κ

Sahidic Version (text is that of Th(ompson); variants in Thompson's apparatus appear
as Th*ᵃᵖᵖ* in the apparatus below the text, where variants found in H(orner) and his
apparatus, H*ᵃᵖᵖ*, are also recorded)

(5.11) ... ΕΕΙΤΑϢΕ ΟΕΙϢ ΜΠCΒΒΕ ΑϨΡΟΙ ΟΝ CΕΔΙϢΚΕ ΜΜΟΕΙ ΕΙΕ ΑϤΟΥϢCϤ Ν̅GΙ
ΠΕCΚΑΝΔΑΛΟΝ ΜΠΕCⲣ̅ΟⲨ̅ (12) ϨΑΜΟΙ ΟΝ ΝΕΥΝΑGϢϪΕ ΕΒΟΛ ΝΝΕΤϢΤΟΡΤⲣ
ΜΜϢΤΝ (13) ΝΤϢΤΝ ΓΑΡ ΝΤΑΥΤΕϨΜ ΘΗΥΤΝ ΕΥΜΝΤΡΜϨΕ ΝΕCΝΗΥ ΜΟΝΟΝ ΤΕΝ-
ΜΝΤΡΜϨΕ ΜΠΡΤΡΕCϢϢΠΕ ΕΥΑΦΟΡΜΗ ΝΤCΑΡΞ ΑΛΛΑ ϨΙΤΝ ΤΑΓΑΠΗ ΜΠΕΠ̅Ν̅Α̅
ΑΡΙ ϨΜϨΑΛ ΝΝΕΤΝΕΡΗΥ (14) ΠΝΟΜΟC ΓΑΡ ΤΗΡϤ ΝΤΑϤϪϢΚ ΕΒΟΛ ϨΝ ΟΥϢΑϪΕ
ΝΟΥϢΤ ϨΝ ΕΚΕΜΕΡΕ ΠΕΘΙΤΟΥϢΚ ΝΤΕΚϨΕ (15) ΕϢϪΕ ΤΕΤΝΛϢΚC ΔΕ ... (22) ...
ΤΑΓΑΠΗ ΠΡΑϢΕ ϯΡΗΝΗ ΤΜΝΤϨΑΡϢ ϨΗΤ ΤΜΝΤΧΡΗCΤΟC ΠΠΕΤΝΑΝΟΥϤ ΤΠΙCΤΙC
(23) ΤΜΝΤΡΜΡΑϢ ΤΕΓΚΡΑΤΙΑ ΝΑΙ ΝΤΕΙΜΙΝΕ ΜΠΝΟΜΟC ϯ ΟΥΒΗΥ ΑΝ (24) ΝΑ
ΠΕΧ̅C̅ ΔΕ Ι̅C̅ ΑΥCⲣ̅ΟⲨ̅ ΝΤCΑΡΞ ΜΝ ΜΠΑΘΟC ΜΝ ΝΕΠΙΘΥΜΙΑ (25) ΕϢϪΕ ΤΝΟΝϨ
ϨΜ ΠΕΠ̅Ν̅Α̅ ΜΑΡΝΑϨΕ ΟΝ ΕΠΕΠ̅Ν̅Α̅ (26) ΜΠΡΤΡΕΝϢϢΠΕ ΝϢΟΥϢΟ ΕΝΠΡΟΚΑΛΕΙ
ΝΝΕΝΕΡΗΥ ΕΝΦΘΟΝΕΙ ΕΝΕΝΕΡΗΥ (6.1) ΝΕCΝΗΥ ΕϢϢΠΕ ΟΝ ΕΡϢΑΝ ΟΥΡϢΜΕ
ΝϨΗΤ ΘΗΥΤΝ Π̣Ϩ ΝϨΕ ϨΝ ΟΥΠΑΡΑΠΤϢΜΑ ΝΤϢΤΝ ΝΕΠΝΕΥΜΑΤΙΚΟC CΒΤΕ ΠΑΙ
ΝΤΕΙΜΙΝΕ ϨΝ ΟΥΠ̅Ν̅Α̅ ΜΜΝΤΡΜΡΑϢ ΕΚGϢϢΤ ϨϢϢΚ ΕΡΟΚ ΜΗΠϢC ΝCΕΠΙΡΑϨΕ ΜΜΟΚ

5.11 ΕΙΕ] Η Η*ᵃᵖᵖ*   Ν̅GΙ] Μ Η*ᵃᵖᵖ*   12 ΕΝΕΥΝΑGϢϪΕ Η   13 ΤΕΤΝΜΝ-
ΤΡΜϨΕ Th*ᵃᵖᵖ*   15 ΤΕΤΝΛϢΚC Η*ᵃᵖᵖ* Th] ΤΕΤΝΑΛϢΚC Η   22 ΠΠΕΤΝΑΝΟΥϤ]
ΜΝΤΠΕΤΝΑΝΟΥϤ Η*ᵃᵖᵖ*   25 ΤΕΤΝΟΝϨ Η*ᵃᵖᵖ*   6.1 ΟΝ om. Η*ᵃᵖᵖ*   ΜΗΠΟ-
ΤΕ Η*ᵃᵖᵖ*

Bohairic Version (text is that of H(orner Boh.); variants recorded in Horner's apparatus are listed below the text)

(5.11) ... ΟΥCΕΒΙ ΟΝ ΠΕϯϨΙ ϢΙϢ ΜΜΟϤ ΙΕ ΕΘΒΕ ΟΥ CΕGΟϪΙ ΝCϢΙ ϨΑΡΑ ΑϤ-
ΚϢΡϤ ΝϪΕ ΠΙCΚΑΝΔΑΛΟΝ ΝΤΕ ΠΙCⲣ̅C ΝΤΕ Π̅Χ̅C̅ (12) ΑΜΟΙ ΝCΕϪϢϪΙ ΕΒΟΛ
ΝϪΕ ΝΗ ΕΤϢΘΟΡΤΕΡ ΜΜϢΤΕΝ (13) ΝΘϢΤΕΝ ΓΑΡ ΝΑCΝΗΟΥ ΑΥΘΑϨΕΜ ΘΗΝΟΥ
ΕΥΜΕΤΡΕΜϨΕ ΜΟΝΟΝ ΜΠΕΡΙΝΙ Ν̅ϯΜΕΤΡΕΜϨΕ ΕϨΟΥΝ ϧΕΝ ΟΥΛϢΙϪΙ ΝΤΕ ϯCΑΡΞ
ΑΛΛΑ ΕΒΟΛ ϨΙΤΕΝ ϯΑΓΑΠΗ ΑΡΙ ΒϢΚ ΝΝΕΤΕΝΕΡΗΟΥ (14) ΠΙΝΟΜΟC ΓΑΡ ΤΗΡϤ
ΑϤϪΗΚ ΕΒΟΛ ϧΕΝ ΟΥCΑϪΙ ΝΟΥϢΤ ϧΕΝ ΦΜΕΝΡΕ ΠΕΚϢΦΗΡ ΜΠΕΚΡΗϯ (15) ΙCϪΕ

ΔΕ ΤΕΤΕΝϬΙ ΛΑΠϹΙ ... (22) ... ΟΥΑΓΑΠΗ ΟΥΡΑϢΙ ΟΥϩΙΡΗΝΗ ΟΥΜΕΤΡΕϤϢΟΥ ΝϩΗΤ
ΟΥΜΕΤΧΡ︦Ϲ︦ ΟΥΜΕΤΑΓΑΘΟϹ ΟΥΝΑϩ︦Ϯ (23) ΟΥΜΕΤΡΕΜΡΑΥϢ ΟΥΕΓΚΡΑΤΙΑ ΝΑΙ
ΜΠΑΙΡΗϮ ΜΜΟΝ ΝΟΜΟϹ Ϯ ΟΥΒΗΟΥ (24) ΝΗ ΔΕ ΝΤΕ Π︦Χ︦Ϲ︦ Ι︦Η︦Ϲ︦ ΑΥΙϢΙ ΝΤΟΥϹΑΡϪ
ΝΕΜ ΝΕϹΠΑΘΟϹ ΝΕΜ ΝΕϹΕΠΙΘΥΜΙΑ (25) ΙϹΧΕ ΔΕ ΤΕΝШΝϩ ϩΕΝ ΠΙΠ︦Ν︦Α︦ ΙΕ
ΜΑΡΕΝϮ ΜΑϮ ΟΝ ΝΕΜ ΠΙΠ︦Ν︦Α︦ (26) ΜΠΕΝΘΡΕΝϢШΠΙ ϩΕΝ ΟΥΜΕΤΜΑΙ ШΟΥ ΕϤ-
ϢΟΥΙΤ ΕΝϹШΚ ΝΝΕΝΕΡΗΟΥ ΕΠϮ ΕΝΕΡ ΦΘΟΝΟϹ ΝΝΕΝΕΡΗΟΥ (6.1) ΝΑϹΝΗΟΥ
ΕϢШΠ ΑΡΕϢΑΝ ΤΟΤϤ ΝΟΥΡШΜΙ Шε ϩΕΝ ΠΑΡΑΠΤШΜΑ ΝΘШΤΕΝ ϩΑ ΝΙΠ︦Ν︦Α︦ΤΙΚΟϹ
ϹΕΒΤΕ ΦΑΙ ΜΠΑΙΡΗϮ ϩΕΝ ΟΥΠ︦Ν︦Α︦ ΜΜΕΤΡΕΜΡΑΥϢ ΕΚΜΟΥϢΤ ΜΜΟΚ ϩШΚ ΜΗΠШϹ
ΝϹΕΕΡ ΠΙΡΑΖΙΝ ΜΜΟΚ

5.11 ΕΘΒΕ ΟΥ ΟΝ   12 ΝΧΕ] Ν   ΕΤϢΘΟΡΤΕΡ] ΕΤΕΡϢΘ.   13 ΓΑΡ] ΔΕ
ϩΕΝ ΟΥΛШΙΧΙ] Ε(Ο)ΥΛ.   ϩΙΤΕΝ om.   ϮΑΓΑΠΗ ΝΤΕ ΠΙΠ︦Ν︦Α︦   15 ΔΕ om.
23 ΟΥΜΕΤΡΕΜΡШΟΥϢ   ΝΑΙ ΓΑΡ   24 ΝΤΕ Π︦Χ︦Ϲ︦ Ι︦Η︦Ϲ︦] ΕΤϩΕΝ Π︦Χ︦Ϲ︦, ΝΤΕ Ι︦Η︦Ϲ︦ Π︦Χ︦Ϲ︦
25 ΔΕ om. ΤΕΝΟΝϩ   ΝΕΜ ΠΙΠ︦Ν︦Α︦] ΜΠΙΠ︦Ν︦Α︦, ΝΕΜ ΝΑ ΠΙΠ︦Ν︦Α︦   26 ΟΥΟϩ
ΜΠΕΝΘ. ΦΘΟΝΟϹ] ΦΘΟΝΙΝ   6.1 ϩΕΝ ΟΥΠΑΡΑΠ.   ΝΘШΤΕΝ ΔΕ   ϩΑ] ϩΕΝ
ΕΚΜΟΥϢΤ] ΕΚΧΟΥϢΤ   ΠΙΡΑΖΙΝ] ϹΦΡΑΓΙΖΙΝ

5.11 ΑϩΑΙ: Till, *Dialektgramm.* §134; also possible is ΕΤΒΕ Ο (Till, *Achmim. Gramm.* §218c Anm.).

N]ϹШΙ: despite the correction (see apparatus), Ш seems certain, and the trace before it is compatible with Ϲ; Μ]ΜΑΙ cannot be read. The space seems better suited to ϹΕΡ ΔΙШΚΕ, modeled on the Sahidic, than to an Achmimic spelling of ϹΕϬΟΧΙ, as offered by the Bohairic. For ΝϹШ= with ΔΙШΚΕ, cf. e.g. Acts 26.11 (Thompson).

ΑΠΕ[ϹΚΑΝΔΑΛΟΝ: the plenum form of the article is rare in Achmimic (Till, *Achmim. Gramm.* §51 B.2), and the short form appears in V 4 (Π︦Χ︦Ϲ︦). The scribe's practice seems to vary, further complicating the task of restoration.

5.12 Because of the uncertainty in reading the letters before ΠШϩ, even an exempli-gratia reconstruction is risky. I have thought of ΕϹΕΠШϩ [ΕΤΟΥϬШΧΕ ΑΒΑΛ ΝΝ]ΕΤϢΤΑΡΤ[Ρ(Ε), "may it succeed that those who disturb you be mutilated." But ΕϹΕ-, though paleographically possible, is surprising instead of Achmimic ΑϹΑ-, and I have not been able to find close parallels to the construction.

ϢΤΑΡΤ[Ρ(Ε): in pure Achmimic we would expect ϩΤΑΡΤΡΕ; Crum lists the spelling with initial Ш only as a noun (*Dict.* 597b).

5.13 Ν]ΑΥΤΑϩΜ: for the Perf. II in Achmimic, see Polotsky, *Rev. Böhlig* 25 and n. 1 (= *Collected Papers* 396).

Ρ-: for Ρ- as an imperative in Achmimic, see, e.g., Prov. 31.4 (Böhlig) Ρ ϩШΒ ΝΙΜ.

ϬΑ[(Ο)ΥΑΝ: this word has not yet appeared in Achmimic; I have used the spelling ϬΑ(Ο)ΥΑΝ, which Crum lists as "S*ᵃ*S*ʲ*A²F" (*Dict.* 835b).

5.14 The restoration [ϩΝ ΟΥϢΕΧΕ, etc. deviates from the word order of the Sahidic and Bohairic version but corresponds to that of the Greek: ὁ γὰρ πᾶς νόμος ἐν ἑνὶ λόγῳ πεπλήρωται.

5.15 ЄІ ТЄ Ш[АТЄТN-: the ample space before Є suggests that a new verse begins here, and ЄІ ТЄ may easily be regarded as a transcription of εἰ δέ, which the Greek has at this point. Ш[АТЄТN- (or ШАРЄТN-) instead of ᴈАРЄТN- may seem unwarranted, but it derives support from ЄТШТАРТ[Р(Є) in R 4. Neither Sahidic ᴧШКС nor Bohairic бІ ᴧАПСІ is attested in Achmimic; therefore even an exempli-gratia restoration of the verb is pointless.

5.22 ТМNТПЄ[ТNАNОУЧ: this reading may be concealed in one of the texts in H^{app}: МNТПЄТNАNОУЧ, i.e. ТМNТПЄТNАNОУЧ?

5.23 МN N[ОМОС, etc.: cf. ММОN NОМОС in the Bohairic.

5.25] .ᴈNЄСЄМ[: the first letter, though damaged, appears to be either М or N, and М seems more suitable to the traces. This cluster of letters corresponds to nothing in the Sahidic or Bohairic version, and I have been unsuccessful in making sense of it. Possibly]М2NЄ is the end of a verb with the 1st person plural suffix, and СЄ could represent NСА (CRUM, Dict. 314a). But the following М remains puzzling.

5.26 ЄЧШОУЄ[ІТ: Є appears to be corrected from А.

6.1] .ШШС: if the text is restored correctly, this probably renders προλημφθῇ ... ἔν τινι παραπτώματι, but I have not been able to discover an appropriate word. The first letter is, most likely, either Ҳ or Х, and if the restoration of the beginning of the verse is accurate, probably no more than two letters preceded].ШШС.

ЄК]МОУᴈ: see CRUM, Dict. 210b.

7

HEBREWS 2.11-15

P. Mich. inv. 4969.2   13.6 × 11.1 cm.   10th cent.

This text is described in Worrell, *Mich.* p. 11 as a "fragment of a paper leaf numbered NZ-NH." It belongs with the large number of fragments obtained together with Mich. MS 158, from the White Monastery (see Worrell p. 5). Paleographically, the text should probably be assigned to the tenth century; cf. the title section of Cramer, *Paläographie* No. 25 (A.D. 903).

I have collated the text with the editions of Horner and Thompson. The only new reading is in V 9 (= Heb. 2.15). Comparison with the textus receptus shows that about six lines are missing between the end of the recto and the beginning of the verso.

Recto

Ⲛ̄Ⲍ̄

ϢⲒⲠⲈ ⲀⲚ ⲈⲘⲞⲨⲦⲈ	2.11
ⲈⲢⲞⲞⲨ ϪⲈ ⲚⲀⲤⲚⲎⲨ	
Ⲉ̄ϤϪⲰ Ⲙ̇ⲘⲞⲤ· ϪⲈ ✝	12
ⲚⲀϪⲰ Ⲙ̇ⲠⲈⲔⲢⲀⲚ	

5   ⲈⲚⲀⲤⲚⲎⲨ· Ⲛ̇ⲦⲘⲎ
     ⲦⲈ ⲚⲦⲈⲔ⟨Ⲕ⟩ⲖⲎⲤⲒⲀ̀ ✝
     ⲚⲀⲤⲘⲞⲨ Ⲉ̀ⲢⲞⲔ·
     ⲀⲨⲰ ⲞⲚ ϪⲈ ⲀⲚⲞⲔ ✝   13
     ⲚⲀϢⲰⲠⲈ ⲈⲒⲚⲀⲌⲦⲈ
10   ⲈⲢⲞϤ· ⲀⲨⲰ Ⲟ̇Ⲛ ϪⲈ
     ⲈⲒⲤ ⳎⲎⲎⲦ[Ⲉ] ⲀⲚ[Ⲟ]Ⲕ Ⲙ̇Ⲛ

_ _ _ _ _ _ _ _

(Ca. 6 lines missing)

Verso

Ⲛ̄Ⲏ̄

ⲀϤⲘⲈⲦⲈϪⲈ ⲈⲚⲀⲒ·	14
ϪⲈⲔⲀⲤ ⲈⲂⲞⲖ ⳎⲒⲦⲈⲚ	
ⲠⲈϤⲘⲞⲨ· ⲈϤⲈⲞⲨⲰⲤϤ̇	
Ⲙ̇ⲠⲈⲦⲈ ⲞⲨⲚⲦϤ̇ ⲠⲀ	

5   ⲘⲀⳎⲦⲈ Ⲙ̇ⲘⲀⲨ Ⲙ̇ⲠⲘⲞⲨ·
     ⲈⲦⲈ ⲠⲀⲒ ⲠⲈ· ⲠⲆⲒⲀ̀ⲂⲞ
     ⲖⲞⲤ· ⲀⲨⲰ ⲚⲈϤⲠⲖⳠ   15
     ⲚⲀⲒ ⲈⲦϢⲞⲞⲠ ⳎⲚ̇ ⲦⲐⲞ

TE Ⲙ̇ⲠⲘⲞⲨ· ⲌⲘ̄ ⲠⲈⲞⲨ

10   ⲞⲈⲓⳲ ⲦⲎⲢⳈ Ⲙ̇ⲠⲈⲨⲀ̀

ⳲⲈ· ⲈⲨⲞ ⲚⲈⲚⲞⲬ[Ⲟ]Ⲥ
.

— — — — — — — —

Collation with H(orner) and Th(ompson) (See above, p. XV)
2.12 ⲈⲚⲀⲤⲚⲎⲨ H^{app}Th^{app}:   ⲚⲚⲀⲤⲚⲎⲨ H, ⳲⲚ ⲚⲀⲤⲚⲎⲨ Th
15 ⳲⲘ ⲠⲈⲞⲨⲞⲈⲓⳲ: ⲘⲠⲈ(Ⲟ)ⲨⲈⲓⳲ HTh

V

1 ⲀⳈⲘⲈⲦⲈⲬⲈ ⲈⲚⲀⲓ: the scribe first wrote ⲀⳈⲘⲈⲦⲈⲬⲈⲓⲚⲀⲓ; he then inserted
a small Ⲉ above the ⲓ of -ⲘⲈⲦⲈⲬⲈⲓ, doubtless in an attempt to cancel the ⲓ.
3 ⲈⳈⲈⲞⲨⳜⳈ: Ⳉ² added above the line.
4 ⲞⲨⲚⲦⳈ: Ⲛ corrected from Ⲉ.
7 ⲚⲈⳈⲠⲗⳄ: i.e. ⲚⳈ- (Conjunctive).

8

REVELATION 18.7-10

P. Mich. inv. 4538c   10.4 × 6.5 cm.   9th cent.

This fragmentary parchment leaf was briefly described in Worrell,
Mich. p. 11.   The recto, numbered ⲘⲐ, contains Rev. 18.7-8; and the
verso, numbered Ⲛ, has Rev. 18.10.   The sheet is broken off at the
bottom, and approximately 17 lines are missing.   Although little of
the text remains, its general style of writing points to the ninth century;
it is rather comparable to Cramer, *Paläographie* No. 19, which is dated
to A.D. 823.

For this section of Revelation, Horner's text rests upon only three
witnesses, two of them damaged (see his apparatus).   Only one manuscript (Horner's siglum: a) gives a rendition of κάθημαι βασίλισσα
καὶ χήρα οὐκ εἰμί (18.7): ⲀⲚⲞⲔ ⳇⲚⲀⳲⲘⲞⲞⲤ ⲀⲚ ⲈⲓⲞ ⲚⲬⲎⲢⲀ.   This is
clearly defective, and collation with the Michigan text (R 1-4) shows

that haplography was responsible: read ⲀⲚⲞⲔ ⲦⲚⲀⲌⲘⲞⲞⲤ ⟨ⲈⲒⲞ ⲚⲢⲢ⳱
ⲚⲦⲚⲀⲌⲘⲞⲞⲤ⟩ ⲀⲚ... There are no other deviations from Horner's edition.

Recto (Flesh Side)

$$\overline{\text{ⲘⲐ}}$$

ⲠⲈⲤⲌⲎⲦ· ⲬⲈ ⲀⲚⲞⲔ·   18.7

ⲦⲚⲀⲌⲘⲞⲞⲤ· ⲈⲒⲞ ⲚⲢ

ⲢⳲ· ⲚⲦⲚⲀⲌⲘⲞ

ⲞⲤ ⲀⲚ· ⲈⲒⲞ· ⲚⲬ[ⲎⲢⲀ]

5   ⲞⲨⲆⲈ ⲚⲦ[ⲚⲀⲚⲀⲨ ⲀⲚ]

ⲈⲌⲎⲂ[Ⲉ ⲈⲦⲂⲈ ⲠⲀⲒ]   8

Ⲍ[Ⲛ ⲞⲨⲌⲞⲞⲨ ⲚⲞⲨⳲⲦ]

———————————

(Ca. 17 lines missing)

Verso (Hair Side)

$$\overline{\text{Ⲛ}}$$

ⲚⲦⲈⲤⲂⲀⲤⲀⲚⲞⲤ· ⲈⲨ   10

ⲬⳲ ⲘⲘⲞⲤ ⲬⲈ ⲞⲨⲞⲒ

ⲞⲨⲞⲒ· ⲚⲦⲚⲞϬ· ⲘⲠⲞ

ⲖⲒⲤ ⲦⲂⲀⲂⲨⲖⳲⲚ

5   ⲦⲠⲞⲖⲒⲤ ⲈⲦⲦⲀⲬⲢⲎⲨ

[ⲬⲈ ⲌⲚ ⲞⲨⲞ]ⲨⲚⲞⲨ· ⲚⲞⲨ

[ⳲⲦ ⲀϤⲈⲒ Ⲛ]ϬⲒ ⲠⲈⲤ

———————————

Collation (see introd.)

V

7 ⲠⲈⲤ: i.e. ⲠⲈⲤ/[ⲌⲀⲠ.

9

GREGORY OF NAZIANZUS, ENCOMIUM
ON BASIL OF CAESAREA

P. Mich. inv. 5567a   20.2 × 13.3 cm.   8th cent.
Louvain Ms. 44 (Lefort)   20 × 19 cm.

This text, a folio from a bicolumnar codex, is composed of two non-contiguous pieces: P. Mich. inv. 5567a preserves the upper part of the sheet; the lower part was in the library of the University of Louvain but was destroyed in the course of World War II. Fortunately, L. Th. Lefort included a description of this second piece as well as a photograph of the recto in his catalogue, *Les Manuscrits coptes de L'Université de Louvain*, Vol. 1 (Louvain 1940) No. 44 (and Pl. X).[1] Professor J. Vergote has kindly informed me (letter of 28 March 1977) that no photograph of the verso has appeared among Lefort's papers, and so we must content ourselves with a partial transcription in the Louvain catalogue (see below). I have transcribed the recto from Lefort's plate.

Lefort dated the writing to the eighth century: he found the style remarkably similar to Schubart, *P. Graec. Berol.* 50 (from the White Monastery; ca. 719) and concluded that, if not written by the same scribe, both texts came from the same scriptorium and were clearly contemporaneous.

The text, as Lefort saw, contains the beginning of a Sahidic translation of the Panegyric of Gregory of Nazianzus on Basil of Caesarea (for the Greek original, see Migne, *PG* XXXVI 493ff). The Coptic translator has often had recourse to loose paraphrase instead of verbatim rendition, and he may not always have understood his model (see note to R ii 31f). The introductory section (R i 1-24), set off by an elaborate border, is a considerable expansion of the Greek title:

---

[1] The connection between the Michigan and Louvain pieces is recorded in E.M. Husselman's unpublished inventory of Coptic papyri. The Louvain text is not mentioned in the description of P. Mich. inv. 5567a in WORRELL, *Mich.* p. 16.

Εἰς τὸν μέγαν Βασίλειον, ἐπίσκοπον Καισαρείας Καππαδοκίας, ἐπιτάφιος (Migne 493.1f).

Because of the nature of the translation, we cannot determine precisely how many lines have been lost between the Michigan and the Louvain pieces, but the amount of missing text was not large and probably did not exceed a few lines (cf. notes on R i 10f and R ii 12f).

A tiny fragment, found in the same envelope as the Michigan section, in fact belongs to the Louvain piece. The recto, which fits on R i 30-32, reads:

```
                    — — — — —
(30)                  ]Ṛ[
                    ]ỴΝΕΒΟΛ[
                    ]ỴΠΟ[
                    — — — — —
```

The verso reads :

```
                    — — — — —
                    ] . . . ＋Ç[
                    ]ΕΤΟΥ[
                    — — — — —
```

To judge from the position of the recto, the two lines of the verso occupy, respectively, the third and fourth lines from the bottom of the second column. Lefort published his transcription of only the end of that column, Ⲛ̄ⲨⲀⲬⲈ ⲆⲈ ⲈⲦⲚⲀⲬⲈⲤⲦ̄Ч ("and the words which will exalt him"), which he connected with Migne 496 line 12. The Greek here reads: line 9 ... ὧν 10 γὰρ τοὺς ἐπαίνους οἶδα, τούτων σαφῶς καὶ τὰς 11ἐπιδόσεις · ἐπ' οὐδενὸς οὖν τῶν ἁπάντων, οὐκ ἔστιν 12ἐφ᾽ ὅτῳ οὐχὶ τῶν ἁπάντων. τοῖς τε λόγοις αὐτοῖς 13ἀμφοτέρωθεν ἂν ἔχοι τὸ πρᾶγμα καλῶς. This is an exceptionally obscure piece of Greek, which the facing Latin translation in Migne thus elucidates: "Quarum enim rerum laudes novi, earum quoque haud dubie incrementa explorata habeo; nec quidquam omnino est, quod non hac ratione augeatur. Postremo, quod ad sermones attinet, utrovis modo res praeclare se habitura est." Lefort's passage, Ⲛ̄ⲨⲀⲬⲈ ⲆⲈ ⲈⲦⲚⲀⲬⲈⲤⲦ̄Ч, seems to be derived from τοῖς τε λόγοις αὐτοῖς, and possibly the first line of the verso fragment should be restored as †C̣[ΟΟΥΝ, i.e. οἶδα.

Recto

	Col. i		Col. ii
			Ā
(Mich.) →	ΟΥΕΓΓΩΜΙΟΝ ΕΑϤ		ἘΧ̄Ν̄ ΝΑϢΑΧΕ Ν̄
	ΤΑΥΟϤ Ν̄ϬΙ ΠΠΕΤΟΥ		ϨΟΥΟ ΕΘΕ ΕΤΕΡΕ ΟΥΑ
	ΛΑΒ ΑΠΑ ΓΡΗΓΟΡΙΟC		ΝΑΡΑϢΕ ΕΧΝ ΝΕϤ
	ΠΘΕΟΛΟΓΟC· ΠΕΠΙC		ϢΑΧΕ Μ̄ΜΙΝ Μ̄
	[Κ]ΟΠΟC ΝΑΖΙΑΝΖΟC	5	ΜΟϤ· ΕϢΑϤΡ̄
	[Ε]ΠΒΙΟC ΜΠΝΟϬ ΒΑ		ΠΑΪ ΔΕ ΜΕϢΑΚ ΕϤ
	[CΙ]ΛΙΟC ΠΕΠΙCΚΟΠΟC		ΓΥΜΝΑΖΕ Μ̄ΜΟΝ
	[Ν]ΤΚΑΙCΑΡΙΑ Ν̄ΤΚΑΠ		ΧΕΚΑC ΕϤΕΤΑΑϤ
	[Π]ΑΔΟΚΙΑ ΕΠΕΙΔΗ		ΝΑΝ Μ̄ΜΙΝ Μ̄
	[Π]ΕϤϢΒΗΡ ΠΕ· Ν̄	10	ΜΟϤ· ΤΕΝΟΥ ϨΩC
	[ΤΑ]ϤΤΑΥΟΥΕ ΠΕΙΕΓ		ΝΟϬ Ν̄ϨΥΠΟΘΕCΙC
	[ΓΩΜΙ]ΟΝ Ν̄[Τ]Ε ΠΕΙ		ΝΑΓΩ[Ν ΕΤ]ΡΕΝ
	[ϢΒΗΡ]Ρ̄ ϨΩΒ ΠΕΪ		[± 7]···
	[± 4]ΕCΟ Ν̄··[		——————————
	[± 6]·[	15	
	——————————		
	——————————		——————————
(Louv.)	···[···]·····		ΕΡϢΑΝ ΟΥΑ ΓΑΡ ΟΥ
	ΠΕϤΜΟΥ· ΕΥΔΙΠΑΙ		ϢϢ ΕΟΥΕΝϨ̄ ΤΕϤ
	ΝΟC ΜΕΝ Μ̄ΠΔΙΚΑΙ		ϬΟΜ ΕΒΟΛ ϨΜ̄ ΠϢΑ
	ΟC· ΑΥΩ ΠΝΟϬ ΕΤΜ̄		ΧΕ ΜΝ̄Ν̄CΩC Ν̄ϒ
	ΜΑΥ ΕΤΒΕ ΝΕϤΑΡΕ	20	ΔΟΚΕΙ ΝΑϤ ΕΡ ΠΑΪ

ΤΗ· ΕΥΝΟϤΡΕ ΔΕ
ΝΑΝ ϨШШΝ ΑΝΟΝ
ΝΕΤϹШΤΜ· ΑΥШ
ΕΥϨΗΥ Ν̄ΝΕΝΨ[Χ]Η ·
ϨΜ ΠΕΥΟΕΙϢ ΕϤϢΟΟΠ   25
ΝΜΜΑΝ ϨΜ ΠϹШ
ΜΑ Ν̄Ϭῑ ΠΕΝΕΙШ[Τ]
Μ̄ΜΑΚΑΡΙΟϹ ΠΝΟϬ
ΒΑϹΙΛΙΟϹ ΝΕϢΑϤ
ΚШ ϨΑΡШΝ ϨΝ̄ ΟΥ   30
ΜΟΥΝ ΕΒΟΛ Ν̄ϨΑ[Ϩ]
Ν̄ϨΥΠΟΘΕϹ[Ι]Ϲ ΕΤ
ΡΕΝϢΑϪΕ ΕΡΟΟΥ
ΝΕϢΑϤΡΑϢΕ ΓΑΡ

ΕϤϬШϢΤ ΕΠϢΙ
ΕΤΕ ΠΑΙ ΠΕ ΝϤ
ΚΑ ΟΥϨΥΠΟΘΕϹ[ΙϹ]
ΝΟΥШΤ Μ̄ΠΕϤ
Μ̄ΤΟ ΕΒΟΛ· ΕΒΟΛ
ϨΝ̄ ΝϨΥΠΟΘΕϹΙϹ
ΤΗΡΟΥ Ν̄ΘΕ ΝΝ
ϨШΓΡΑΦΟϹ ΕΤ
ϬШϢΤ̄ ΕΜ̄ΠΙ
ΝΑΞ· ΤΜΕΕΥΕ ΔΕ
ϪΕ ΤΑΪ ΤΕΤΕ[ϤΝΑ]
ϹΟΥΤΟΝϤ [ΕϨΟΥΝ]
ΕΡΟϹ· ϨШϹ Ε[ΙϬΟ Ν]
ϢΟΡΠ̄ ΕΝΚΟΟΥΕ

Verso

Col. i

(Mich.) ↑ B̄ ΑΥШ ΕϹΟΥΟΤϤ ΕΠϢΑ
ϪΕ· ΤΑΪ ΤΕ ΘΕ ΕΟΥ
ΝΟϬ Ν̄ϨШΒ ΠΕ ϢΑ
ϪΕ ΕΠΤΑΪΟ Μ̄ΠΕΙ
ΡШΜΕ· Η̄ ΝΑϨ   5
ΡΑΝ ΑΝ Μ̄ΜΑΤΕ
ΝΑΪ Ν̄ΤΑΥΚΑΤΑ
ΦΡΟΝΕΙ Μ̄ΠΤΑ
ΙΟ̄ Μ̄ΠΕΙΡШΜΕ

Col. ii

Η̄ ΕΙΝΑΤΟΥΝΕϹ
ΠϢΑϪΕ ΕϨΡΑΪ ϨΝ̄
ΟΥ· ΕΙΜΗΤΕΙ ϨΙ
ΤΜ̄ ΠΤΑΪΟ Μ̄Π[ΕΙ]
ΡШΜΕ· ΑΝΟΚ   5
ΜΕΝ ΓΑΡ ΟΥΧ[ΡΕ]
ШϹ ΝΑΪ ΠΕ Π[ΑΪ]
ΕΙΝΑϢ ΜΑϨϤ
ΠϢΑϪΕ ΔΕ Π[Ε]

ⲀⲖⲖⲀ ⲚⲀⲊⲢⲚ̄ Ⲛ̄   10   ⲬⲢⲈⲰⲤ ⲈⲦⲦ[
ⲔⲞⲞⲨⲈ ⲞⲚ ⲈⲦⲈⲢⲈ   .ⲊⲚⲞⲨ[
ⲠⲈⲨ[ⲰⲚⲊ] Ⲛ̄[[.]ⲦⲀⲒ̈Ⲟ Ⲛ̄[
Ⲫ[————————————

———————————

(*R i*; *Mich.*) An encomium which the holy Apa Gregory, the theo-
logian and the bishop of Nazianzus, pronounced concerning the life
of the great Basil, the bishop of Caesarea in Cappadocia, since he was
his friend; he pronounced this encomium of this fellow-worker, this ...
(*Louv.*) ... his death, on the one hand for praise of that just and great
man on account of his virtues, on the other for a benefit to us as
well, we who hear, and for a profit to our souls.

In the time when our blessed father, the great Basil, was with us in
the body, he would set before us continually many subjects for us to
speak about. For he would rejoice (*R ii*; *Mich.*) over my words
more than one would rejoice over his own words. And perhaps he
did this in training us that he might give us his own self now as a great
subject of discourse for us to ... (*Louv.*) For if one wishes to manifest
his ability in speech, and afterwards it seems good to him to do this
in looking to the measure, that is, (if) he places a single subject before
himself from all the subjects, just like the painters who look to the
pictures — I think that it is to this that he will direct himself, as it
takes precedence over the others (*V i*; *Mich.*) and surpasses speech.
Thus it is a great thing to speak of the honor of this man, not only
for ourselves, who have made light of the honor of this man (*sic*), but
also for the others whose life ... (*V ii*) Or in what shall I exalt the
speech except through the honor of this man? For, as far as I am
concerned, this is an obligation for me, if I can discharge it. But,
as for the speech, the debt which ...

R i
     5 ⲚⲀⲌⲒⲀⲚⲌⲞⲤ: i.e. ⲚⲚⲀⲌⲒⲀⲚⲌⲞⲤ; see Kahle, *Bala'izah* I 112f.
     10f Ⲛ[ⲦⲀ]ⲨⲦⲀⲨⲞⲨⲈ: probably Perf. II; if the emphasis lies on ⲈⲨⲀⲒⲠⲀⲒⲚⲞⲤ

ΜΕΝ ... ΕΥΝΟϤΡΕ ΔΕ, lines 17ff, then not much text has been lost in the lacuna after line 15.

13 [ϢΒΗΡ]Ρ: better suited to the lacuna than ϢΒΡΡ-; for the spelling, cf. e.g. Rom. 16.9 (Horner).

ΠΕΙ: also possible is ΤΕΙ.

24 I have not attempted to reproduce the ornate border beneath this line; see the plate in Lefort (Pl. X).

30-32 The writing in these lines is badly damaged, and the reading, though inspired by the Greek original, is not certain. In line 30, ΚШ (= προτιθείς; Migne 493.4) is particularly difficult, but a form of +, which renders προθήσειν (Migne 493.6) below, R ii 8, cannot be read.

R ii

12f Perhaps ΕΤ]ΡΕΝ[ϢΑΧΕ ΕΡΟϹ (cf. R i 32f); there is no room for ΝΑΙ ΕΤΕ]ΡΕ Ν- or even ΝΕΤΕ]ΡΕ Ν-, which would initiate a relative phrase corresponding to the Greek τοῖς περὶ λόγους ἐσπουδακόσιν (Migne 493.7f). These words may have been rendered in the lines now lost in the lacuna. At the end of line 13 there are unidentifiable traces, probably of two letters, followed by a medium punctum.

25 ΕΒΟΛ ΕΒΟΛ: repetition of ΕΒΟΛ is rare; cf. e.g. Luke 9.8 (Horner).

30 ΔΕ: apodotic ΔΕ.

31f I.e. ΤΕΤϤΝΑϹΟΥΤШΝϤ. For the phrase, cf. BUDGE, *Miscell. Texts* 339 (in CRUM, *Dict.* 372a) +ΝΑϹΟΟΥΤΝ ΜΠΑΟΥШϢ ΕϨΟΥΝ ΕΡΟΚ. In lines 30 - V i 2, the Coptic translator appears to have misunderstood the original: the Greek (οἶμαι ... ταύτην ἂν ὑφελὼν μόνην, ὡς λόγου κρείττονα, τῶν ἄλλων ἑλέσθαι τὴν πρώτην; Migne 493.8-13) seems to mean: "I think ... that he would have set this one apart, as surpassing oratory, and would have chosen the first of those remaining."

V i

5 Η seems to be redundant; it is perhaps the result of a corruption of μὴ ὅτι γε in the original (Migne 493.14).

9 ΜΠΕΙΡШΜΕ: a seemingly inappropriate addition; the Greek (Migne 493.14f) has ἡμῖν τοῖς πάλαι πᾶν τὸ φιλότιμον καταλύσασιν. The addition may have been the fault of the scribe, not of the translator: note that here and in line 4, ΜΠΕΙΡШΜΕ is preceded by ΠΤΑΙΟ.

12f Ν and Φ appear to be the best interpretation of the traces (the supralinear stroke over the first is visible), but I can offer no convincing restoration of these lines, which should render οἷς βίος ἐστὶν ὁ λόγος (Migne 493.15f). There may be room for [ШΝϨ Ϩ]Ν or Ο]Ν.

V ii

1ff The column begins with a loose translation of the Greek: ἢ ὅ τί ποτ' ἂν μᾶλλον ... χαρισαίμην ... τοῖς λόγοις αὐτοῖς, ἢ τὸν ἄνδρα τοῦτον θαυμάσας (Migne 496.3-5).

10-12 I have not succeeded in restoring these lines. The lacuna at the end of line 10 can hold up to three letters; ЄⲦⲦ[suggests either ЄⲦⲦⲞ ("to require") or ЄⲦ (relative marker) followed by a verb beginning with Ⲧ. The first letter in the following line appears to be either Є or Ⲃ; Ⲣ is also possible, though less likely. The Greek has χρέος δέ, εἴπερ ἄλλο τι, τοῖς ἀγαθοῖς τά τε ἄλλα καὶ περὶ τὸν λόγον, ὁ λόγος (Migne 496.6-8).

10

HYMNS TO THE ARCHANGEL MICHAEL

P. Mich. inv. 4567a   13.3 × 13.6 cm.   11th cent.

This text is briefly described in Worrell, *Mich.* pp. 13f: "Inv. 4567a is a complete parchment folio ... containing liturgical hymns to St. Michael the archangel. The hand resembles that of P. Berl. 9287, and the orthographic and grammatical peculiarities are the same as those discussed by Junker ["Koptische Poesie des 10. Jahrhunderts," *Oriens Christianus* 6 (1906) 403-411[1]]. There are seven complete strophes and an incomplete strophe at the beginning and the end of the leaf."

As is generally the case with Coptic hymns, the text is written continuously; the end of a verse is marked with a medium punctum, that of a stanza with ⸗ (usually with ·7 in the margin[2]), and that of a section with :— (thrice absent: R 13, 18; V 19). Each section is sepa-

---

[1] This work I cite in the three-volume issue which appeared in *Oriens Christianus*: I—6 (1906) 319-411; II—7 (1907) 136-253; III—8 (1911) 2-109. I have not used the two-volume reprint which appeared under the same title in Berlin, 1908-1911. For a photograph of P. Berl. 9287, see I Tafel 1.

[2] The ·7 is absent in R 6 and in V 10, in both cases perhaps because of physical damage to the sheet. In the last strophe on the recto, it has been placed opposite line 22, because the large initial letter at the beginning of line 20 necessitated its transposition; in the edition I put it beside 21.

rated from the following by a broken line,[3] and each begins with instructions for its performance (see note to R 3).

Coptic hymns are normally divided into pairs of stanzas of an equal number of verses (Junker I 347). The present text displays this patterning in R 10-13 (3 + 3),[4] 15-18 (3 + 3), V 2-6 (4 + 4), and 14-19 (4 + 4), but elsewhere there are irregularities: R 4-9 (3 + 4), 20-24 (2 + 4), V 8-12 (4 + 5). Two of these (R 20-24 and V 8-12) may be easily corrected,[5] but if R 4-9 is to conform to normal practice, more drastic surgery is needed: if ΠЄΧЄ ΦΙЄΡΟΨΑΛΤΗϹ ΔΔΔ is a gloss, and the ⸗ sign is placed after ΜΙΧΑΗΛ (cf. R 11, 17), we are left with 3 + 3. Junker discusses similar anomalies in I 350-352 and on 372 notes "dass wir keine absolute Garantie für die korrekte Ueberlieferung des Textes haben."[6]

Despite the predominantly Sahidic base, at times vocalization associated with Fayumic appears: ΟΥΑΝ (R 15), ЄΜΑϤ (V 4), and ΧΑΡЄ, i.e. ΧЄ ΑΡЄ (R 18 and V 19). Note also the pervasive substitution of Є for Ν, the various manifestations of which are listed in Junker I 406f. This substitution is likewise characteristic of Sahidic — especially vulgar Sahidic — with Fayumic influence: see No. 13 in this volume, introd. p. 52.

In terms of paleography, the Michigan text should probably be assigned to the same period as P. Berl. 9287 mentioned above, i.e. to the eleventh century of our era (cf. Crum, Review of Junker I, in *Orientalistische Literaturzeitung* 9 [1909] 397).

For other hymns to Michael, see M. Cramer, *Koptische Hymnologie in deutscher Uebersetzung* (Wiesbaden 1969) 92-103.

---

[3] The breaks are irregular, and for ease of typesetting, I have substituted a continuous line.
[4] The colon after ΝЄΠΗΥЄ I take to be a sign of punctuation, not a verse marker.
[5] If in R 21 we shift the ⸗ sign after ЄΠΟΚ, we have 3 + 3, and if we delete the punctum after ΧЄ at the end of V 10, the result is 4 + 4.
[6] See also III 34 n. 1 and 54 n. 1.

Recto (Flesh Side)

ⲚⲦⲞⲔ ⲀⲔⲠⲰⲦ ϢⲀ ⲆⲀⲚⲒⲎⲖ· ⲈϤⲤⲈ

ⲠⲈⲤⲎⲦ ⲈⲠϢⲎⲒ ⲈⲚⲈⲘⲞⲨⲒ· ⲀⲔⲦⲞⲨⲬⲞϤ ⲘⲠⲈ

ⲠⲈⲐⲞ[ⲞⲨ] ⲦⲀⲌⲞϤ:- | ⲠⲞⲨ̄· ⲤⲦⲞⲬ ⲞⲚ·

ϢⲀⲢⲈ ⲠⲀⲄⲄⲈⲖⲞⲤ ⲘⲠϬ̄Ⲥ· ⲔⲰⲦⲈ ⲈⲚⲈⲦⲈ̄Ⲣ

5   ⲌⲞⲦⲈ Ⲛ̄ⲌⲎⲦϤ· ⲠⲈⲬⲈ ⲪⲒ̄Ⲉ̄ⲢⲞⲮⲀⲖⲦⲎⲤ

Ⲇⲁⲇ̄= ⲠⲀⲢⲬⲀⲄⲄⲈⲖⲞⲤ ⲘⲒⲬⲀⲎⲖ· ⲚⲦⲞϤ

ⲠⲈⲦⲔⲰⲦⲈ ⲈⲠⲒⲖⲀⲞⲤ· ⲈϤⲤⲞⲠⲤ̄ ⲈⲠⲈⲬ̄Ⲥ̄

Ⲉ̄ⲬⲰⲚ· Ⲛ̄ϤⲔⲀ ⲚⲈⲚⲚⲞⲂⲈ ⲚⲀⲚ Ⲉ̄ⲂⲞⲖ:-

ⲤⲦⲞⲬ ⲞⲚ

10   ⲀⲒⲚⲀⲨ ⲈⲨⲬⲰϢⲢⲈ ⲚⲀⲄⲄⲈⲖⲞⲤ· ⲌⲈ ⲚⲈⲠⲎⲨⲈ:

·7   Ⲁ̇ⲚⲞⲔ ⲒⲰ̄ ⲀⲒⲘⲞⲨⲦⲈ Ⲉ̄ⲠⲈϤⲢⲀⲚ ⲬⲈ ⲘⲒⲬⲀⲎⲖ=

ⲈϤϢϢ ⲈⲂⲞⲖ ⲬⲈ ⲖⲀⲞⲤ ⲚⲒⲘ· Ⲁ̄ⲢⲒ ⲌⲞⲦⲈ Ⲛ̄ⲌⲎ

ⲦϤ ⲈⲠϬ̄Ⲥ Ⲉ̄ⲚⲈϬⲞⲘ· ⲬⲈ ⲠⲈϤⲚⲀ ⲘⲎⲚ ⲈⲂ[Ⲟ]Ⲗ ⲈϢⲀ [Ⲉ]ⲚⲈⲌ

ⲤⲦⲞⲬ ⲞⲚ

15   ⲞⲨⲀⲚ Ⲍ̄ ⲚⲀⲢⲬⲎⲀⲄⲄⲈⲖⲞⲤ· ⲔⲰⲦⲈ ⲠⲈⲐ

ⲢⲞⲚⲞⲤ Ⲉ̄ⲠⲈⲦⲞⲚⲌ̄· Ⲡ̄ⲚⲞϬ ⲈⲦⲈⲚⲌⲎⲦⲞⲨ ⲠⲈ ⲘⲒ

·7   ⲬⲀⲎⲖ= ⲚⲦⲞϤ ⲈⲦⲤⲞⲠⲤ ⲈⲠⲈⲦⲞⲚⲌ̄· ⲬⲈ ⲀⲢⲒ ⲞⲨ

ⲚⲀ ⲘⲈ ⲚⲈϢⲎⲢⲈ ⲚⲀⲆⲀⲘ· ⲬⲀⲢⲈ ⲠⲈⲨⲢⲞⲞⲨϢ ⲚⲎⲬ ⲈⲢⲞⲔ

ⲠⲞⲨ̄· ⲤⲦⲞⲬ ⲚⲒⲘ ⲠⲈ ⲠⲤⲞⲪⲞⲤ ⲈⲢⲈⲘⲈⲌ⳯

20   ⲈⲢⲈ ⲚⲒⲘ ⲦⲚ̄ⲦⲰⲚ Ⲉ̄ⲢⲞⲔ· ⲘⲒⲬⲀⲎⲖ ⲠⲀ ⲠⲢⲀⲚ

·7   ⲈϢ[Ⲟ]Ⲩ ⲦⲀⲒⲞϤ= Ⲁ̄ⲠⲈⲦⲞⲚⲌ̄ ⲚⲀⲨ Ⲉ̄ⲢⲞⲔ· ⲈⲔⲞ Ⲛ

ϢⲀⲚⲀⲌⲦⲎϤ· ⲀϤⲔⲀⲀⲔ ⲈⲔⲌⲒ ⲞⲨⲚⲀⲘ ⲈⲘⲞϤ·

ⲈⲔⲤⲞⲠⲤ̄ ⲌⲀ Ⲡ̄ⲄⲈⲚⲞⲤ ⲈⲚⲀⲆⲀⲘ:-

Verso (Hair Side)

ⲠⲞⲨ· ⲤⲦⲞˣ ⲚⲦⲞ ⲦⲈ ⲠⲦⲞⲞⲨ ⲈⲦⲭⲞⲤⲈ
ⲘⲀⲢⲈ ⲚⲀ ⲘⲠⲎⲨⲈ ⲞⲨⲚⲞϤ· ⲚⲦⲈ ⲚⲀ ⲠⲔⲀⲌ ⲦⲎ
ⲢϤ ⲦⲈⲖⲎⲖ· ⲈⲦⲂⲈ ⲘⲓⲭⲀⲎⲖ· ⲭⲈ ⲀⲠ͞Ϭ͞Ⲥ Ⲥⲱ

·7 ⲠⲦ ⲈⲘⲀϤ⸗ ⲀϤⲦ ⲚⲀϤ Ⲉ͞ⲠⲈⲭⲢ[Ⲟ] ⲘⲈ ⲦⲈϬⲞⲘ·

5 ⲈϢⲞⲨϢⲞⲨ ⲈⲦⲦⲀⲓⲎⲨ· ⲀϤⲔⲀⲀϤ ⲈϤⲤⲞⲠⲤ ⲘⲘⲞϤ·
ⲭⲈ ⲚⲀ ⲌⲀ ⲠⲄⲈⲚⲞⲤ ⲈⲚⲀⲆⲀⲘ:-

ⲤⲦⲞˣ ⲞⲚ

ⲀⲒⲚⲀⲨ ⲈⲨⲚⲞϬ ⲚϢⲠⲎⲢⲈ· ⲠⲀⲒϢⲦ [Ⲛ]ⲦⲈⲓⲠⲞⲖⲒⲤ
Ⲉ͞ⲠⲞⲞⲨ· Ⲙ͞Ⲛ ⲞⲨⲢⲀϢⲈ ⲈϤⲠⲞⲢϢ ⲈⲂⲞⲖ· ⲘⲀ

10 ⲦⲀⲘⲞⲒ ⲭⲈ ⲞⲨⲚ͞ⲦⲈ ⲠⲈⲒⲌⲰⲂ⸗ ⲠⲈⲭⲀϤ ⲭⲈ·
ⲠⲀϢⲎⲢⲈ· ⲠⲀⲒ ⲠⲈ ⲠⲚⲞϬ ⲘⲘⲒⲭⲀⲎⲖ· ⲈϤⲤⲞⲠ͞Ⲥ
Ⲉ͞ⲠⲈⲦⲞⲚ͞Ⲋ· ⲭⲈ ⲚⲀ ⲌⲀ ⲠⲄⲈⲚⲞⲤ Ⲛ͞ⲚⲀⲆⲀⲘ:-

ⲠⲞⲨ̄ ⲤⲦⲞˣ ⲭⲈⲢⲈ ⲠⲤⲞⲖⲤⲖ ⲈⲚⲀⲄⲄⲈⲖⲞⲤ
ⲈⲠⲤⲀ Ⲙ͞ⲠⲈⲌⲖⲞϬ ⲈⲘⲒⲭⲀⲎⲖ· ⲈϤⲤⲈ ⲦⲘⲎ

15 ⲦⲈ Ⲛ͞ⲚⲀⲄⲄⲈⲖⲞⲤ· Ⲉ͞ⲢⲈ ⲦⲈϬⲢⲎⲠⲈ ⲌⲒⲭⲈ
·7 ⲦⲈϤⲀⲠⲎ· Ⲉ͞ⲢⲈ ⲠⲈⲌⲢⲀⲂⲦⲞⲤ ⲌⲈ ⲦⲈϤϬⲒⲭ⸗
ⲭⲈ ⲚⲦⲞϤ ⲈⲦⲌⲒ ⲞⲨⲚⲀⲘ Ⲙ͞Ⲡ͞Ⲥ͞Ⲱ͞Ⲣ· ⲈϤⲤⲞⲠⲤ
ⲘⲘⲞϤ ⲚⲞⲨⲞⲈⲒϢ ⲚⲒⲘ· ⲭⲈ ϢⲀⲚⲀⲌⲦⲎⲔ ⲌⲀ
ⲦⲈⲔⲌⲒⲔⲰⲚ· ⲭⲀⲢⲈ ⲠⲈⲨⲢⲞⲞⲨϢ ⲚⲎⲭ ⲈⲢⲞⲔ

---

20 ### ⲤⲦⲞˣ ⲞⲚ

ⲠⲈⲔⲢⲀⲚ ⲌⲞⲖϬ̄ ⲈⲨⲦⲀⲨⲞ̄ Ⲙ͞ⲘⲞϤ· ⲠⲀⲢⲭⲀⲄ
ⲄⲈⲖⲞⲤ ⲘⲒⲭⲀⲎⲖ· ⲘⲈ ⲠⲈⲔⲔⲈϢⲂⲎⲢ
·7 Ⲉ̇ⲖⲒⲦⲞⲨⲢⲄⲞⲤ· ⲄⲀⲂⲢⲒⲎⲖ ⲠϤⲀⲒ ϢⲈⲚⲞⲨⲂⲈ⸗

R

You went to Daniel,
when he was down in the pit of the lions,
and you saved him before evil befell him.

    Manner: same

The angel of the Lord
seeks those who fear Him,
says the temple-singer David.
The archangel Michael:
he it is who seeks this people,
as he entreats Christ on our behalf,
that He may forgive us our sins.

    Manner: same

I saw a mighty angel
in the heavens, I, Iohannes,
and I called his name Michael,
as he shouted out: "Every nation,
fear the Lord of powers,
because His mercy continues forever."

    Manner: same

Seven archangels
surround the throne of the Living One.
The greatest amongst them is Michael.
He it is who entreats the Living One (saying):
"Be merciful with the sons of Adam,
because it is upon You that their care rests."

    Manner: Who is the one wise and intelligent?

Who is like you,
Michael, you of the praiseworthy name?
The living One saw you
in your mercy,
and He let you be at His right hand,
as you entreated concerning the race of Adam.

V

    Manner: It is you who are the lofty mountain.
Let those of the heavens rejoice,
and let those of the entire earth be glad
concerning Michael,
because the Lord has chosen him.
He has given him the might and the power,
proud and honored,
and He let him entreat Him (saying):
"Be merciful concerning the race of Adam."
    Manner: same
I saw a great marvel,
my father, in this city today,
and a widespread joy.
Tell me what this thing is.
He said:
"My son, this is the great Michael,
entreating the Living One (saying):
' Be merciful concerning the race of Adam.' "
    Manner: Rejoice, consolation of the angels.
As regards the beauty of the sweetness of Michael:
he is in the midst of the angels,
the diadem is on his head,
the staff is in his hand,
because he it is who is at the right hand of the Saviour,
entreating Him always (saying):
"Be merciful concerning Your likeness,
because it is upon You that their care rests."
    Manner: same
Your name is sweet as it is uttered,
archangel Michael,
and your fellow-servant as well,
Gabriel, the bringer of good tidings

R

1f Cf. Junker III 106.15f ⲀⲤⲚⲞⲨⲤⲘ ⲚⲆⲀⲚⲒⲎⲖ ⲈⲨⲘⲠⲈⲤⲎⲦ ⲈⲠⲰⲎⲒ ⲈⲚⲈⲘⲞⲨⲒ.

2 ⲈⲚⲈⲘⲞⲨⲒ: i.e. ⲚⲘⲘⲞⲨⲒ; for ⲚⲈ- instead of Ⲛ-(Ⲙ-), see Junker I 410; so elsewhere in this text: R 10 (ⲚⲈⲠⲎⲨⲈ), 13 (ⲈⲚⲈⲄⲞⲘ), 18 (ⲚⲈⲨⲎⲢⲈ).

2f Cf. Junker II 194.8 ⲈⲠⲈ ⲖⲀⲀⲨ ⲈⲠⲈⲐⲞⲞⲨ ⲦⲀⲤⲞⲚ; 198.3 ⲘⲠⲈ ⲠⲈⲐⲞⲞⲨ ⲦⲀ[ⲤⲞ]Ⲥ.

3 Note that the line beneath this strophe is raised to show that ⲠⲞⲨ· ⲤⲦⲞˣ ⲞⲚ· goes with the following.

ⲠⲞⲨ· ⲤⲦⲞˣ: i.e. ⲠⲞⲨⲰⲤⲘ ⲤⲦⲞⲬⲞⲤ; according to Junker I 346, "Es bezeichnet ⲤⲦⲞⲬⲞⲤ = στοῖχος, στίχος den Bau der Strophe und ihren Rhythmus, und ⲞⲨⲰⲤⲘ die Melodie." (ⲤⲦⲞⲬⲞⲤ may be correct as it stands: see E. WELLESZ, *A History of Byzantine Music and Hymnography*, 2nd Ed. [Oxford 1961] 73f.) ⲤⲦⲞⲬⲞⲤ seems to be the more comprehensive of the two terms: it can be used without ⲠⲞⲨⲰⲤⲘ in this text and elsewhere, and in such cases it appears to include the meaning of the latter (R 9, 14; V 7, 20; see Junker I 346f). In my translation, I have followed Junker and have rendered ⲠⲞⲨ and ⲤⲦⲞˣ together as "manner" (Junker: "Weise").

ⲞⲚ: here means "same," as contrasted with those hymns whose musical elements are different from the preceding (R 19; V 1, 13); cf. ⲀⲖⲖⲞⲤ ⲞⲚ, Junker I 342.

4-9 On the possibility that these verses are corrupt, see above, introd.

8 ⲚⲨⲔⲀ: here equivalent to a final clause (TILL, *Gramm.* §323). In a purely continuative sense, the conjunctive is not used after a circumstantial present or a second present (POLOTSKY, *Conjugation System* 402 [= *Collected Papers* 248]). For its "subjunctive" use after these tenses, cf. GARITTE, *Vita Antonii* 97.11f ϮⲚⲀⲨ ⲄⲀⲢ ⲈⲢⲞⲒ ⲈⲢⲈ ⲠⲬⲞⲈⲒⲤ ⲔⲀⲖⲈⲒ ⲘⲘⲞⲒ ⲦⲀⲂⲰⲔ ⲰⲀⲢⲞⲨ (cf. 121 ii 11-14 ϮⲚⲀⲨ ⲄⲀⲢ ⲈⲢⲞⲒ ⲈⲢⲈ ⲠⲬⲞⲈⲒⲤ ⲘⲞⲨⲦⲈ ⲈⲢⲞⲒ ⲈⲨⲔⲀⲖⲈⲒ ⲘⲘⲞⲒ ⲈⲦⲢⲀⲂⲰⲔ), REYMOND-BARNS, *Coluthus* 26 (90 R i 13f) ⲘⲎ ⲈⲔⲰⲒⲠⲈ ⲚⲄⲤⲞⲘⲞⲖⲞⲄⲈⲒ ("are you ashamed to admit it?" — editors' translation, p. 146).

13 [Ⲉ]ⲚⲈⲤ: added below the line.

15f ⲔⲰⲦⲈ ⲠⲈⲐⲢⲞⲚⲞⲤ: despite the uncertainty of the second epsilon, which may have been corrected, the reading appears to be preferable to the expected ⲔⲰⲦⲈ ⲈⲠⲈⲐⲢⲞⲚⲞⲤ (ⲔⲰⲦⲈ Ⲉ-: R 4, 7); for a precise parallel, see Junker III 20.10 ⲈⲨⲔⲰⲦⲈ ⲈⲠⲈⲐⲢⲞⲚⲞⲤ ⲈⲠⲈ... (read ⲈⲠⲈⲦⲞⲚⲤ?).

17 ⲚⲦⲞⲨ ⲈⲦⲤⲞⲠⲤ: abbreviated cleft sentence, as in V 17 ⲚⲦⲞⲨ ⲈⲦⲤⲒ (contrast R 6f ⲚⲦⲞⲨ ⲠⲈⲦⲔⲰⲦⲈ); see POLOTSKY, *Nominalsatz* 424f (= *Collected Papers* 429f), and cf. Ps. 21.29 (Budge) ⲚⲦⲞⲨ ⲈⲦⲞ ⲚⲬⲞⲈⲒⲤ (αὐτὸς δεσπόζει), 43.22 (Bu.) ⲚⲦⲞⲨ ⲄⲀⲢ ⲈⲦⲤⲞⲞⲨⲚ (αὐτὸς γὰρ γινώσκει).

ⲞⲨ: the parchment has ϫ; see H. QUECKE, "Die Schreibung des ⲞⲨ in koptischen Handschriften," *Archiv für Papyrusforschung* 22 (1973) 277f.

18 ⲨⲎⲢⲈ: Ⲏ corrected from Ⲛ.

ⲬⲀⲢⲈ etc.: cf. Junker II 160.8 ⲈⲢⲈ ⲠⲀⲢⲞⲞⲨ[Ⲩ ⲚⲎⲬ Ⲉ]ⲢⲞⲨ (= Ps. 55 [54] 23: see Junker *ad loc.*), 224.4 ⲬⲈ ⲈⲢⲈ ⲠⲈⲚⲢⲞⲞⲨⲨ ⲚⲎⲬ Ⲉ[ⲢⲞⲨ]. For the elision of

ⲬⲀⲢⲈ (=ⲬⲈ ⲀⲢⲈ), cf. Junker I 408. ⲈⲢⲞⲔ is inserted beneath the line. The same phrase occurs in V 19.

19 ⲈⲢⲈⲘⲈⳅⲎⲦ: i.e. ⲚⲢⲘⲚⳅⲎⲦ; cf. Junker II 142.22 ⲈⲢⲈⲘⲚⳅⲎⲦ; 148.9 ⲈⲢⲈⲘⲈⳅⲎⲦ.

20 ⲈⲢⲈ ⲚⲒⲘ ⲦⲚⲦⲰⲚ ⲈⲢⲞⲔ: cf. Junker III 50.22 [Ⲉ]ⲢⲈ ⲚⲒⲘ ⲦⲚⲦⲰⲚ ⲈⲢⲞⲔ; for the second tense with interrogative pronouns as actors, see POLOTSKY, *Études* 51f (= *Collected Papers* 155f), *Conjugation System* 409 (= *Coll. Pap.* 255).

21 The stanza sign should probably be placed after ⲈⲢⲞⲔ: see above, introd. n. 5.

22 ⲀⳓⲔⲀⲀⲔ ⲈⲔ-: note the auxiliary/causative use; also in V 5. See CRUM, *Dict.* 95b.

23 ⲈⲚⲀⲀⲘ i.e. ⲚⲀⲀⲘ (also in V 6).

V

3f ⲤⲰⲠⲦ: i.e. ⲤⲰⲦⲠ.

8 [Ⲛ]ⲦⲈⲒⲠⲞⲖⲒⲤ: Ⲛ for ⳅⲚ (cf. K. PIEHL, "Études coptes," *Sphinx* 5 [1902] 89-92).

10 ⲞⲨⲚⲦⲈ: I cannot construe this as it stands, and I assume that it is corrupt for ⲞⲨ ⲠⲈ.

ⲠⲈⲬⲀⳓ ⲬⲈ·: the medium punctum should probably be deleted; see above, introd. n. 5.

11 ⲘⲘⲒⲬⲀⲎⲖ: i.e. ⲘⲒⲬⲀⲎⲖ; cf. ⲚⲚⲀⲀⲘ for ⲚⲀⲀⲘ in the following line.

14 ⲈⲠⲤⲀ: a similar Ⲉ- appears at the beginning of a verse in Junker III 54.1 ⲈⳅⲈⲚⲤⲒⲞⲨ ⲈⲨⲢ ⲞⲨ⟨Ⲟ⟩ⲈⲒⲚ (in 60.14, ⲈⲔⲈⲤⲘⲞⲨ = ⲚⲔⲈⲤⲘⲞⲨ). This is probably the preposition Ⲉ-, used in the loose sense of "as regards."

16 ⳅⲢⲀⲂⲦⲞⲤ: i.e. ῥάβδος.

23 ⲠⳓⲀⲒ ⳉⲈⲚⲞⲨⲂⲈ: i.e. ⲠⳓⲀⲒ ⳉⲘⲚⲞⲨⳓⲈ (CRUM, *Dict.* 570b); cf. KROPP, *Lobpreis* 219 ⲄⲀⲂⲢⲒⲎⲖ ⲠⲂⲀⲒ ⳉⲈⲚⲞⲨⲂⲒ. -ⲂⲈ⳽ is inserted below the line.

11

EARLY BOHAIRIC TEXT

P. Mich. inv. 4162   4.8 × 6.5 cm.   5th or 6th cent.

This papyrus is briefly described in Worrell, *Mich.* p. 20, and a pen drawing of the recto, copied from a photograph, appears in the same volume on Plate IV. The description reads: "Another Bohairic fragment worthy of mention, although it is very small and has not been identified, is Inv. 4162. It contains the words ⳉⲈⲚ, [Ⲉ]ⲐⲞⲨⲀⲂ, ⲘⲠⲀⲒⲢⲎ†, and on paleographical grounds could certainly not be dated

later than the sixth century. The hand, indeed, might well be dated
earlier ...'' In the unpublished inventory, under Inv. 4162 we read:
"Miscellaneous fragments including one from an early Bohairic Coptic
codex, V-VI at the latest. Unidentified text, mentions ⲀⲄⲄⲈ[ⲖⲞⲤ],
ⲢⲀⲪⲀ[ⲎⲖ].'' Because of its early date, I publish a transcript of this
text here — together with a photograph of both sides — although I too
have been unable to identify it. Assignment of recto and verso is
totally arbitrary, and since so little survives, the precise articulation
of individual words remains in doubt. The appearance of the adjec-
tive ⲠⲀⲦⲢⲒⲔⲎ (R 1) in a text which mentions the archangel Raphael
(V 8f) may be significant: the island of Patres is known to be associated with Raphael,[1] and ⲠⲀⲦⲢⲒⲔⲎ may refer to that island. Possibly
we should restore ⲠⲀⲦⲢⲒⲔⲎ Ⲛ[ⲎⲤⲞⲤ, although I cannot parallel this
particular designation of the island.

Recto

→   ⲠⲀⲦⲢⲒⲔⲎⲚ[
     ⲀⲔⲰⲀⲚⲞⲨⲰ[
     ⳃⲈⲚⲞⲨⲐⲀⲨ[
     ⲐⲎⲤⲀⲨⲢⲞ[Ⲥ
5   ⲦⳃⲈⲚⲦⲈⲔ[
     ⲈⲦⲈⳃⲀⲚ[
     ⲘⲠⲀⲒⲢⲎ┼[Ⲁ]
     ⲚⲞⲔⲀⲀ́/[
     ·[
     — — — — — — — — — —

[1] See Tito ORLANDI, "Un encomio copto di Raffaele Archangelo," *Rivista degli Studi Orientali* 47 (1974) 215.

Verso

↑   ]Ν†ΝΟΥ / ΝΤΕ

             ]ΝΕΤΧΑ

             ] ·ΑΚϧΕΝ

             ]ΤΑϥΟΥΟΡ

5   ]ΑΠΙΑΓΓΕ

[ΛΟC   ]ΜΜΟΚΕϨΡΑΝ

             ]ΕΘΟΥΑΒ /

             ]ΓΑΡΡΑΦΑ

[ΗΛ   ] . . [

— — — — — — — — —

R

3 ΕΝ: Ν corrected from Ο.

8 ΔΔ: this may stand for the Greek δεῖνα δεῖνος, or it may be an abbreviation for ΔΑΥΕΙΔ. In the former case, we may be dealing with a magical text, in which such expressions often occur (see KROPP, *Zaubertexte* II i ad 21, ii ad 1). ΔΛ, i.e. ΔΑΝΙΗΛ, is paleographically less likely.

V

4 ΟΥΟΡ[: e.g. ΟΥΟΡΠ=, from ΟΥΩΡΠ (CRUM, *Dict.* 489a).

6 ΕϨΡΑΝ: probably ΕϨΡΑ=Ν, "to us."

12

CHRISTIAN AMULET

P. Mich. inv. 1559   5.9 × 10.8 cm.   7th or 8th cent.

This text is mentioned in Worrell, *Mich.* p. 18 as "an amulet on vellum, containing the titles and first words of each of the four Gospels, with magical symbols at the bottom." Such amulets were valued in antiquity for their magical efficacy; for a discussion, with bibliography, see Kropp, *Zaubertexte* III 210 paragraph 359. See also Jernstedt, *Push.* 36.

The Michigan piece is written in a crude, unpractised style, with little attention to word division between lines. Paleographically it exhibits some similarities with *Mich.* III 10, plate VI, No. 6864, (middle of 7th cent.) and *OMH* 61, plate I (7th/8th cent.). Note the tendency to substitute Є for N: ЄКАТА 8 and 12 (cf. NКАТА 2 and 5), ЄGI 14; and ЄN for N: ЄNЄNШAХЄ 11, ЄNA2PN 15f. This phenomenon is common in vulgar Sahidic texts with Fayumic influence; see No. 13 below, p. 52.

(Hair Side)

ПЄYANГЄΛION ЄTOY

ΛΛB NKATA MAӨA)

ПХШШМЄ NПЄХПO N

Ī͞C ПЄХ͞C [П]ШHPЄ NΔΛΛ

5   ПЄYAГГЄΛION NKATA M

ΛPK/ TAPX[H] NПЄY

ΛГГЄΛION N[Ī͞C] ПЄХ͞C

ПЄYAГГЄΛION ЄKATA

ΛOYK⌒ ЄПIΔHПЄ

10   P Є2Λ2 2I TOOT⟨O⟩Y

ЄC2AI ЄNЄNШAХЄ

ПЄYAГГЄΛION ЄKATA I͞Ш

2N TЄ2OYITЄ NЄBШ

OOП ЄGI ПШAХЄ AYШ П

15   ШAХЄ NЄBШOOП ЄNA2P

N ПNOYTЄ

(Magic Signs)

The Holy Gospel according to Matthew. The book of the gener-
ation of Jesus the Christ, the son of David.

The Gospel according to Mark. The beginning of the Gospel of
Jesus the Christ.

The Gospel according to Luke. Since many have undertaken to
write the words.

The Gospel according to John. In the beginning was the Word,
and the Word was in the presence of God.

(Magic Signs)

10 Є-: i.e. ⲗ-; the same spelling occurs in other amulets: *Leyd.* 478.10f ⲈⲠⲒⲆⲎⲠⲈⲢ
ⲈⲌⲀⲌ ⲌⲒ ⲦⲞⲞⲦⲞⲨ; MURRAY, *Osireion at Abydos* XXV 2 (see p. 39) ⲈⲠⲒⲦⲈⲠⲈⲢ
ⲈⲌⲀⲌ ⲌⲒ ⲦⲰⲦⲞⲨ.

13

KALANDOLOGION*

P. Mich. inv. 590   13.3 × 17.5 cm.   Late 9th cent.

The present piece consists of a single leaf from a parchment codex;
each page contains one column of writing 18 lines in length. In general,
the state of preservation is good: there are several small holes and
some surface abrasion, but the only extensive damage occurs in the
upper inner corner, where a lacuna has removed up to five letters per
line (in R 1-3 and V 1-3). See the description in Worrell, *Mich.* p. 20.

The text belongs to the class of subliterary manuals which predict
events on the basis of the Kalends of January. These manuals are
well known in Greek: the so-called καλανδολόγια; and many of them
are cited and transcribed in the *CCAG*.[1] In Coptic, besides the present
Michigan text, the following two examples have thus far appeared:

* A version of the introduction to this text was presented as a lecture at the XVᵉ
Congrès International de Papyrologie (Brussels), on 1 September 1977.

[1] References to texts from the *CCAG* and other pertinent material will be cited in

1) A Vienna parchment codex preserved under several inventory numbers and published by Till, *Bauernpraktik*. It is a series of un-numbered folios to which Till assigned the letters A to P. In addition to the kalandologion (Folio B Verso 9 - Folio F Recto 10), this manual contains related prognostic treatises; see the summary of its contents in Till 110-115. A photograph of the end of the kalandologion may be found in his Tafel 26a.

2) Vienna papyrus K 5506, a fragmentary sheet also published by Till, *Bemerkungen* 329-334.

Till assumed that the first Vienna text[2] consisted of a series of predictions based on the coincidence of 6 Tubi, i.e. 1 January, with each of the seven days of the week (Sunday through Saturday); to this series was added an appendix on 11 Tubi.[3] Here is a schematic outline of the kalandologion, based on Till's edition:

B V 9   Heading [ⲘⲘⲀⲈ]ⲓ̣ⲛ ⲚⲤⲞⲨ ⲤⲞⲞⲨ̣ [ⲈⲦ]ⲰⲂⲈ, "the signs of 6 Tubi" (i.e. 1 Jan.)

　10f   [ⲈⲢⲰ]Ⲁ̣ⲛ ⲤⲞⲨ ⲤⲞⲞⲨ ⲈⲦⲰⲂⲈ ⲬⲰⲰⲤⲈ [ⲈⲦⲔⲨⲢⲒ]ⲀⲔⲎ, "if 6 Tubi falls upon Sunday." Predictions follow.

C   A very badly damaged sheet, on which only a few letters survive. Till assumed it contained predictions if 6 Tubi fell upon Monday and Tuesday.[4]

D R 11   ⲈⲢ[ⲰⲀⲛ ⲤⲞⲨ ⲤⲞⲞⲨ ⲈⲦⲰⲂⲈ ⲬⲰⲰⲤⲈ] .[, "if 6 Tubi falls upon..." This section Till referred to Wednesday. Wednesday's account continues for an unspecified number of lines, and by the time we reach E R we are dealing with Thursday.

E R 11   ⲈⲢⲰⲀⲛ ⲤⲞⲨ ⲤⲞ̣[ⲞⲨ ⲈⲦⲰⲂⲈ ⲬⲰⲰⲤⲈ] ⲈⲠⲞⲨⲰⲤ, "if 6 Tubi falls upon Friday." In his commentary ad loc., Till equated ⲞⲨⲰⲤ with Friday; but see below, p. 51 n. 14.

---

the commentary; for general bibliography; see W. and H. G. GUNDEL, *Astrologumena* (Wiesbaden 1966) 56 n. 9.

[2] Unless otherwise noted, all subsequent references will be to this text (TILL, *Bauernpraktik*).

[3] TILL, *Bauernpraktik* 111.

[4] *Bauernpraktik* 136.

E V 6 [ЄРШⲀN СОУ СОО]У ЄТШШВЄ ХШШВЄ [, "if 6 Tubi falls upon ..."
Till refers this part to Saturday.

F R 3 An appendix which begins ЄРШⲀN ОУНВТ ЄІ ЄВОⲖ NСОУ МNТОУЄ
NТШВЄ. Till could not elucidate the meaning of -НВТ;
his translation reads: "Wenn am 11. Tobe ein ... heraus-
kommt..."

F R 10 Conclusion ⲀУХШК ЄВОⲖ N6І ММⲀЄІN NСОУ СООУ ЄТ̣ШШВЄ, "the
signs of 6 Tubi are completed"

Because of the terribly fragmentary condition of the Vienna kalandologion, Till should be congratulated for getting as much out of it as
he did. Fortunately, the present Michigan text partially overlaps the
Vienna piece in content and is much better preserved. It has accordingly
been of great assistance in furthering our understanding of the Vienna
kalandologion.

The Michigan text unfolds its prognostic advice depending on how
the wind blows from 6 to 10 Tubi;[5] in the midst of its account of 10
Tubi, the sheet breaks off. A few extracts will show its structure:

R 15-17 ЄРШⲀN ПТНУ NⲀНВТ ШШПІ NСОУН̄ NТШВЄ, "if the east wind
comes on 8 Tubi." Predictions follow. (On the spelling НВТ, see
below, note on R 6f.)

V 7-9 ЄРШⲀN ОУТОУ РНС ЄІ ЄВОⲖ N2Ⲁ ШШРП NСОУō̄ NТШВЄ, "If a
south wind comes forth on 9 Tubi." Predictions follow.

V 15-16 ЄРШⲀN ОУⲀМNТ ЄІ ЄВОⲖ NСОУī NТШВЄ, "if a west (wind)
comes forth on 10 Tubi." Predictions follow. (On the spelling
ⲀМNТ, see below, note on V 15.)

These extracts permit a solution to one of Till's problems. In F R 3,
quoted above, ЄРШⲀN ОУНВТ ЄІ ЄВОⲖ NСОУ МNТОУЄ NТШВЄ, Till could
make no sense out of -НВТ: he thought it might stand for ЄІ4Т, "nail,"
perhaps in its metaphorical meaning, "wart."[6] In his review of the
Bauernpraktik,[7] W. Hengstenberg suggested that НВТ was a spelling

---

[5] The reference to 6 Tubi has to be restored; see below, note on R 3.
[6] *Bauernpraktik* 137.
[7] *BZ* 37 (1937) 190.

of ⲈⲒⲂ, "claw." Semantically none of the solutions seems particularly satisfying: "if a nail, wart, or claw comes forth on 11 Tubi" —
this may make sense to some; to me, I must confess, it is bizarre at
best.

Let us now return to the Michigan text. We see that the style be-
comes increasingly more compressed: from ⲠⲦⲎⲨ ⲚⲀⲎⲂⲦ ("the east
wind"), we pass to the construct form of ⲦⲎⲨ, ⲞⲨⲦⲞⲨ ⲢⲎⳅ ("a south
wind"), and finally we come to the total omission of the noun, ⲞⲨⲀⲘⲚⲦ,
literally, "an (instance of the category) west," i.e. a west wind. Similarly, in the Vienna kalandologion, ⲞⲨⲎⲂⲦ must mean "an (instance
of the category) east," i.e. an east wind. This construction, in which
the noun is subordinated to the indefinite article, in a kind of genitive
relationship, is fairly widely attested in Coptic. Consider, for example,
Psalm 77.26, where ⲞⲨⲦⲞⲨ ⲢⲎⳅ (νότον) is followed by ⲞⲨⲈⲘⲚⲦ (λίβα).
Both Jernstedt and Polotsky have discussed similar examples.[8] The
vulgar spelling ⲎⲂⲦ for ⲈⲒⲈⲂⲦ may have confused Till, and he may
not have been familiar with the construction: at least he does not refer
to it in his *Koptische Grammatik* (except perhaps allusively in par. 100).

The section beginning in F R 3 with ⲈⲢⲰⲀⲚ ⲞⲨⲎⲂⲦ ⲈⲒ ⲈⲂⲞⲖ ⲚⳅⲞⲨ
ⲘⲚⲦⲞⲨⲈ ("if an east [wind] comes forth on 11 Tubi") was regarded by Till as a kind of appendix (see above, p. 46 n. 3). As
now elucidated, it appears to be the end of a section detailing the occurrence of winds for the days 6 to 11 Tubi. Though not from the
same codex as P. Mich. inv. 590, the section of the Vienna kalandologion should be regarded as a direct continuation of the Michigan text,
which concerns 6 to 10 Tubi.

At this point, we begin to question Till's reconstruction of his
Vienna text. Our scepticism increases when we see that the two pieces
are often similar in content. This similarity suggests that sections
which Till thought referred to days of the week in fact detail prognosti-
cation by winds. As an example, consider Folio D V 1-4, which, ac-

---

[8] See POLOTSKY, *Coptic* 565, with references to Jernstedt's work; cf. also G. M.
BROWNE, "The Martyrdom of Paese and Thecla," *Chronique d'Egypte* 49 (1974)
204.

cording to Till, belongs to the section dealing with predictions if 6 Tubi falls upon Wednesday. The manuscript is badly abraded and lacunose at this point, and Till could read only parts:[9]

N. [   ] ..ⲁ

ⲛⲉⲭⲧ ..ⲟ.ⲉ...(.) ⲟⲩⲛ[..]ⲙⲁⲗⲉⲑⲉ

ⲛⲧⲧⲁ.... ⲛⲣⲱⲙⲉ ⲛⲁ[ⲙⲟⲩ (?) ⲥⲉ]ⲛⲛⲟⲅ

ⲛⲩⲱⲛⲉ ⲛ[ⲁⲩⲱⲡⲉ   ]ⲟⲩ

Even in this transcription, the Vienna text displays similarities with a section in the Michigan kalandologion; I refer to V 1-6, a series of events which will happen if there is an east wind on 8 Tubi (Note that similarities between the two texts have been underlined):

<u>ⲛⲉⲧⲃⲛⲟⲟⲩⲉ</u>

[ⲛⲁ<u>ⲛⲁⲭ</u>] <u>ⲥ</u>ⲏⲧⲟⲩ ⲃⲟ<u>ⲗ</u>· ⲛ<u>ⲉ</u>ⲥⲟⲩ<u>ⲁ</u>

[ⲛⲁ<u>ⲩⲁ]ⲁ</u>· ⲛ<u>ⲑ</u>ⲏ ⲙⲡⲧⲉⲡⲉⲛ

ⲛⲉⲣⲱⲙⲉ ⲛⲁ<u>ⲩⲁⲡ</u> ⲥ<u>ⲛ</u>ⲛ<u>ⲟⲅ</u> ⲉ

<u>ⲩ</u>ⲱⲛⲉ· ⲛ<u>ⲉⲩ</u>ⲏⲣ<u>ⲉ</u> ⲩ<u>ⲏ</u>ⲙ ⲛ<u>ⲁ</u>

<u>ⲙⲟⲩ</u> [10]

"... the cattle will miscarry, the wheat will become as dry (?) as cumin, the men will suffer severe illnesses, and the children will die."

A photograph of the Vienna text, kindly provided by Dr. H. Loebenstein, showed me that in fact it is almost a duplicate of the Michigan piece. I here present a revision of the lines in question:

ⲛⲉⲧⲃ[ⲛ]ⲏ ⲛⲁ

ⲛⲉⲭ ⲥⲏⲧⲟⲩ ⲉⲃ[ⲟ]ⲗ· ⲛⲉⲥⲟⲩⲟ [ⲛⲁ]ⲩⲁ ⲛⲑⲉ

ⲛⲡⲧⲁⲡⲉⲛ· ⲛⲣⲱⲙⲉ ⲛⲁⲩⲡ ⲥⲛⲛⲟⲅ

ⲛⲩⲱⲛⲉ· ⲛ[ⲉ]ⲩ[ⲏ]ⲣⲉ ⲩ[ⲏ]ⲙ ⲛⲁⲙⲟⲩ

---

[9] In his edition, Till used an asterisk (*) to indicate a letter which he found completely illegible; this I have replaced with the more conventional dot.

[10] On [ⲛⲁⲛⲁⲭ] and [ⲛⲁⲩⲁ]ⲁ, see the commentary ad locc.

Because of these similarities in content, it is only reasonable to assume that this portion of the Vienna text, like that from Michigan, deals with predictions if there is an east wind on 8 Tubi; it does not concern itself, as Till thought, with the coincidence of 6 Tubi with Wednesday.

There are other points of contact between the two texts,[11] and they all point to the same conclusion: Till's kalandologion is in fact two separate treatises. The first concerns prognostications connected with the coincidence of 6 Tubi with days of the week, and the second details predictions based on the kind of wind which blows from 6 to 11 Tubi.

An appendix which I print after the Michigan text provides a revision of the relevant portion of Till's treatise. Here I content myself with a brief summary of the kalandologion as now reconstructed (N.B. pertinent references to P. Mich. inv. 590 have also been added):

Treatise 1

If 6 Tubi falls on Sunday: B V 10ff
If 6 Tubi falls on Monday: C
If 6 Tubi falls on Tuesday: C
If 6 Tubi falls on Wednesday:[12] C - E R 10
If 6 Tubi falls on Thursday (ⲟⲩⲱⲱ): E R 11 - V 5
If 6 Tubi falls on Friday: E V 6-16

Treatise 2

If wind comes on 6 Tubi: E V 17 - D R 10 (Cf. Mich. R 3f)[13]
If wind comes on 7 Tubi: D R 11-15 (Cf. Mich. R 8-14)[13]
If wind comes on 8 Tubi: D R 16 - V 5 (Cf. Mich. R 15 - V 6)
If wind comes on 9 Tubi: D V 6-13 (Cf. Mich. V 7-14)

---

[11] Compare especially Mich. V 8-14 (9 Tubi) and Till D V 6-12; because of their similarity, I have restored 9 Tubi in D V 7. Further, though badly damaged, the remnants of D V 14-16 display affinities with Mich. V 15-17. For further details, see below, pp. 62f.

[12] Till assumed that C concerned only Monday and Tuesday (see above, p. 46 and n. 4), but if the sequence C E D is correct — as I argue below —, C will also have contained at least the beginning of Wednesday's account.

[13] See note to Mich. R 3.

If wind comes on 10 Tubi: D V 14 - F R 2 (Cf. Mich. V 15-18)
If wind comes on 11 Tubi: F R 3-9

Saving details for the commentary to the appendix, I should here make two fairly general observations about the reconstruction: 1) As I stated above, Till equated ⲟⲩⲱϣ (E R 12) with Friday; additional evidence later led him to conclude that it could refer only to Thursday.[14] Unfortunately, he never made the necessary adjustments in the Vienna kalandologion. 2) In the text as reconstructed, I have reversed the sequence of the two folios D and E. Till himself admitted that he was uncertain about the order,[15] and the evidence of the Michigan text shows that E must precede D. Much of E belongs to the first type of kalandologion: we have a reference to Thursday on the recto (ⲉⲣϣⲁⲛ ⲥⲟⲩ ⲥⲟ[ⲟⲩ ⲉⲧⲱⲃⲉ ⲭⲱϣϥⲉ] ⲉⲡⲟⲩⲱϣ, E R 11-12), and though the day is lost in a lacuna, there is similar phraseology on the verso ([ⲉⲣϣⲁⲛⲥⲟⲩ ⲥⲟⲟ]ⲩ ⲉⲧⲱϣⲃⲉ ⲭⲱϣⲃⲉ [, E V 6-7). On the other hand, as has been shown above, there are numerous textual affinities between D and the Michigan text; these affinities show that D, like the Michigan kalandologion, belongs to the second type of treatise.

Each type of kalandologion deals with 6 days, and perhaps they were meant to complement each other. It may seem odd to us that Saturday is excluded from the first type of treatise, especially since the Greek kalandologia regularly extend from Sunday to Saturday.[16] Perhaps the best explanation for its absence will emerge from Till's comment on the section dealing with 11 Tubi (F R 3-9); this is the section that Till regarded as an appendix to the kalandologion (see above, p. 46 n. 3). To explain the relevance of 11 Tubi, he wrote (following a suggestion of Stegemann): "Der 11. Tobe ist der 6. Jänner, der stets im religiösen Leben von Ost und West eine grosse Bedeutung hatte. Da er einmal das Geburtsfest Christi war, erhält er, wenigstens im Westen, für den Aberglauben beinahe die Bedeutung des 1. Jänner.

---

[14] *Wochentagsnamen* 103f, 108; *Bemerkungen* 331.
[15] *Bauernpraktik* 136.
[16] *CCAG* VII 126, VIII 3.191f, X 151f.

Der deutsche Volksglaube ist noch heute voll von Zukunftsdeutung aus diesem Tage, aber auch Ernteweissagungen und Glücksvoraussagen fehlen nicht...; im Orient wird das kaum anders gewesen sein."[17]

I have already mentioned that Type 1 finds analogues in the Greek kalandologia; for a close parallel to type 2, I have nothing in Greek, but a text from the Latin West is rather comparable. I refer to Paris, Bibliothèque Nationale Nouv. acq. 1616, fol. 12v., an unpublished piece which, according to Thorndike,[18] contains "predictions for the ensuing year ... according as there is wind in the night of Christmas eve and the eleven nights following." Here are two extracts, transcribed from a photograph of the manuscript: "Si in nocte fuerit ventus in nocte natalis domini nostri Iesu Christi, in hoc anno reges et pontifices peribunt ... si in nocte xii fuerit ventus, reges et bello peribunt." Doubtless both the Latin text and its Coptic analogues go back to a Greek prototype.

* * *

As regards the date and dialect of the Michigan text, it is quite similar to Till's *Bauernpraktik*, which he assigns to the late ninth century (108) and characterizes as being written in a vulgar Sahidic with Fayumic influence (115). Note especially NE- for N- (plural article): R 10f, 13, V 4f, 11; E- for N-: V 4; final I instead of E: R 5f; OH (= ΘE) R 4, V 3; ⲰNAϨ R 10; OYAN R 17; COYA V 2; NAX- V 13 (restored in V 2); ⲰAⲠ- V 4. In reference to NAX- and ⲰAⲠ-, Till's comment on similar forms in his *Bauernpraktik* is applicable: "... die halbenttonten Formen des status nominalis mit dem Tonvokal ⲁ sind nicht subachmimisch, sondern mit Beeinflussung durch den entsprechenden status pronominalis ... zu erklären." (116) Similarly, NETBNAYE (R 10), rather than being Subachmimic, seems to be a crypto-Fayumic defor-

---

[17] *Bauernpraktik* 137.

[18] L. Thorndike, *A History of Magic and Experimental Science* (New York 1923) 678f. A critical edition, by S. Eriksson, of the Latin calendologia is in preparation, according to E. Svenberg, *Lunaria et zodiologia latina*, Studia Graeca et Latina Gothoburgensia 16 (Gothenberg 1963) 13 n. 1.

mation of ΝΕΤΒΝΟΟΥΕ: a perhaps subconscious compromise on the part of the scribe between Sahidic ΝΕΤΒΝΟΟΥΕ (which appears in V 1 and 12) and "pure" Fayumic ΝΕΤΒΝΑΥΙ. Other anomalous or unusual forms are discussed in the commentary.

Recto (Hair Side)

ϨΙ̇ ΠΑΡΜ̇ϨΑΤ· ΠΝΕϨ· Π̣[ΕϢΑϤ]
ϪΩϤ· ϨΙ̇ ΠΑΡΜ̄ϨΑ̇Τ [± 5]
————————————[
ΠΑ̇Ι ΠΕ ΠϹΙ̇ΜΙ̇ΟΝ· ΝϹΟΥ[Ϛ̄ ΝΤΩ]
ΒΕ· ΕΤΒ̇Ε ΘΗ̇ ΕΤΟΥΤΑΜΟΝ
[Ε]ΝΕΤΡ ΝΟΒΡΙ̇ ΝΑΝ ΜΠΑΤΟΥ
ϢΩ̈ΠΙ̇· ΕΡϢΑΝ ΠΤ̄ΗΥ ΝΑ
ΕΒΤ ΕΙ̇ ΕΒΟΛ ΜΠΕϨΟΟΥ· ΕΤΜ̇
ΜΑΥ· ΝΑΝΟΥ ΠΜΟΟΥ· ΑΥΩ
ϢΑϤϪΙ̇ ΜΠϨΟ ΜΠΚΑϨ ΤΗΡϤ
ΝΕΤΒ̄ΝΑΥΕ ΝΑΩ̈ΝΑϨ· ΝΕ
ΚΑΡΠΟϹ ΝΑΑΥΞΑΝΕ· ΝΕϬΩΜ
ΝΑϮ ΟΥ̇Ω· ΠΕΒΙ̇Ω ΝΑ
ΕΡ ΚΟΥΙ̇· ΘΑΗ ΝΝΕΚΑΡ
ΠΟϹ ΝΤϹΩϢΕ ΝΑΤΑΚΟ
————————————
ΕΡϢΑΝ ΠΤΗΥ ΝΑΗΒΤ
ϢΩΠΙ̇ ΝϹΟΥΗ̄ ΝΤΩ
ΒΕ· ΟῩΑΝ ΟΥΝΟϬ ΝΧΙ̇
ΜΩ̈Ν· ΝΑϢΩΠΙ̇· ΝΑΗΡ

Verso (Flesh Side)

[NAN]OYOY· NETB̄NOOŸE

[NANAϪ] ϨHTOY BOⲨ· NECOYⲀ

[NAϢA]Ⲁ· NⲐH MⲠTEⲠEN

NEPⲰME NⲀϢⲀⲠ ϨⲚNOϬ E

5   ϢⲰNE· NEϢHPE ϢHM NA

MOY·

EⲢϢAN OYTOȲ PHC Eⲓ EBOⲨ

NϨA ϢⲰPⲠ NCOYⲞ̄ NTⲰ·

BE· TE ⲠTHY NEMϨⲓT Eⲓ E

10   BOⲨ ϨA POYϨE· OYNOϬ NϢM ⲠE

NEKⲀPⲠOC NAAYⲜANE· NE

KOYⲓ NTB̄NOOYE NA

NAϪ ϨHTOY BOⲨ AⲨⲨA MEY

·ⲰCK· ⲠEBⲓϢ NAEP ϢAY

---

15   EⲢϢAN OYAMNT Eⲓ EBOⲨ NCOY

Ī NTⲰBE· NTE ⲠTOY

PHC Eⲓ EBOⲨ ϨA POYϨE· OYⲀ

N OYNOϬ MⲠ[P]Ϣ KNⲓ· NA

(R) ... in Phamenoth; the oil will be costly in Phamenoth...

This is the sign of 6 (?) Tubi concerning the way in which we are taught what is profitable to us before it happens. If the east wind comes forth on that day, the water is good, and it will cover the entire earth; the cattle will live, the crops will increase, the gardens will blossom, the honey will diminish, and the last of the crops of the field will perish.

If the east wind comes on 8 Tubi, there will be a great winter, the weather (V) will be good, the cattle will miscarry, the wheat will become as dry (?) as cumin, the men will suffer severe illnesses, and the children will die.

If a south wind comes forth on the dawn of 9 Tubi, and the north wind comes forth at evening, it means a great summer, the crops will increase, the small livestock will miscarry but will not continue (to do so), and the honey will become profitable.

If a west wind comes forth on 10 Tubi, and the south wind comes forth at evening, there will be a long winter of fatness (?) ...

R

1f These two lines may belong to the end of an account which began: "if 6 Tubi falls upon a Friday..." (see above, introd. p. 50); but the corresponding section in TILL's *Bauernpraktik*, E V 6-16, offers nothing comparable.

2I: i.e. 2N? See e.g. JUNKER, *Koptische Poesie* I 404 and 407, and cf. Till G V 6 2N TEKAⲠE and L R 3 2I T[EKA]ⲠE.

ⲠAⲢM2AT: i.e. ⲠAⲢM2OTⲠ (Φαμενώθ), 25 February - 26 March. For the spelling, see CRUM, *Dict.* 269a.

ⲠNE2· Ⲡ[EⲨA4]XⲰ4: also possible, if the line is as short as line 15, is ⲠNE2· N[A]XⲰ4; the faint trace of ink before the lacuna is too faint to permit a decision. XⲰ4 is an alternative spelling of XOY4, "to be costly;" see CRUM, *Dict.* 796a and TILL, *Bemerkungen* 328f. For the cleft sentence, cf. Till F R 13 AⲨ ⲠEⲨA4XOY4.

3 CIMION: i.e. σημεῖον.

NCOY[Ⲋ̄: the restoration NCOY[Z̄ would conform to the sequence elsewhere observable in this text: NCOYH̄ in R 16, NCOYO̅ in V 8, and NCOYĪ in V 15f. But lines 4-6 (ETBE ... MⲠATOYⲨⲰⲠI) constitute a kind of heading, and I therefore believe that this is the beginning of a new section: hence I prefer NCOY[Ⲋ̄. It is possible that the predictions in 8-14 refer to 6 Tubi; but if so, we might expect them to correspond to the account of 6 Tubi in TILL's *Bauernpraktik* (D R 1-10), especially since V 1-6 (8 Tubi) correspond to Till D V 1-4, and V 10-14 (9 Tubi) to D V 6-12. I therefore regard it as more likely that the scribe inadvertently went from the protasis concerning 6 Tubi (lines 6-8) to predictions belonging to 7 Tubi (lines 8-14). But since Till D R 11-15, which ought to concern 7 Tubi, are so damaged, certainty is not possible.

4f ETOYTAMON: the last three letters are damaged but not doubtful; for the M, of which only a small amount of ink remains, cf. the M in V 13 (MEY-). According to the Stern-Jernstedt Rule (see POLOTSKY, *Conjugation System* 401f [= *Collected Papers* 247f]), we expect ETOYTAMO MMON, but in the case of TAMO, a sufficient number of violations have appeared to suggest that the rule does not always apply to this verb: *Push.* 11.3 **+ⲦⲀⲘⲞⲔ**, *Ryl.* 317 **ⲦⲓⲦⲀⲘⲞⲔ**, and a Fayumic fragment published by Gaselee, *JThS* 11 (1910) 514: **ⲈⲨⲦⲀⲘⲘⲀϤ**.[1] All three of these passages have been emended by Jernstedt (see *Push. ad loc.*), but the additional evidence of the Michigan text suggests that **ⲦⲀⲘⲞ** could tolerate object suffixes in the Bipartite Conjugation. (For other violations of the Stern-Jernstedt Rule, cf. e.g. **ⲈϤⲦⲚⲦⲰⲚϤ** in Orlandi, *Phif e Longino* 60.25, 66.17, and see Nagel, *Grammat. Untersuch.* §62:a.)

6f **ⲚⲀⲈⲂⲦ**: i.e. **ⲚⲈⲓⲈⲂⲦ**; in R 15 we find **ⲚⲀⲎⲂⲦ** (cf. Till F R 3 **ⲞⲨⲎⲂⲦ**; for the construction, see above, introd. p. 48. I can parallel neither spelling, but as a glance at Crum's entry (*Dict.* 76b) will show, the word appears in so many orthographic variants that **ⲀⲈⲂⲦ** and **ⲀⲎⲂⲦ** are hardly surprising; for the **Ⲁ**, cf. Fayumic **ⲀⲓⲎⲂⲦ**, listed in Crum.

8 **ⲠⲘⲞⲞⲨ**: i.e. the inundation of the Nile; see Crum, *Dict.* 197b, and cf. Till E V 2 **ⲠⲘⲞⲞⲨ ⲘⲠⲈⲓⲈⲢⲞ**.

9 **ⲰⲀⲨⲬⲓ ⲘⲠⲌⲞ**: "it will cover;" cf. Leipoldt, *Sinuthii vita bohairice* 51.11 (cited by Crum, *Dict.* 647b) **ⲀϤⲐⲢⲈ ⲠⲓⲘⲰⲞⲨ Ⲓ ⲚⲦⲈϤϬⲓ ⲠⲌⲞ ⲘⲠⲓⲔⲀⲌⲓ**.

10 **ⲚⲈⲦⲂⲚⲀⲨⲈ**: see above, introd. pp. 52f.

11 **ⲚⲀⲀⲨⲜⲀⲚⲈ**: **Ⲩ** inserted above the line.

11f **ⲚⲈϬⲰⲘ ⲚⲀ+ ⲞⲨⲰ**: cf. *CCAG* X 152.14 οἱ κῆποι εἰς εὐφορίαν.

12f **ⲠⲈⲂⲓⲰ ⲚⲀⲈⲢ ⲔⲞⲨⲓ**: cf. the Vienna kalandologion, K 5506 R 7 (ed. Till, *Bemerkungen* 333) **ⲠⲈⲤⲞⲨⲞ Ⲛ[ⲀⲢ] ⲔⲞⲨⲓ**.

17 **ⲚⲞϬ**: probably "long," rather than "severe" (the latter meaning is appropriate in V 4), since it is hard to associate a severe winter with the good weather mentioned in the next lines (**ⲚⲀⲎⲢ [ⲚⲀⲚ]ⲞⲨⲞⲨ**; see note to 18f). Cf. K 5506 R 10 (above, preceding note) **ⲦⲈⲠⲢⲰ Ⲛ[Ⲁ]Ⲣ ⲔⲞⲨⲓ**. The phrase **ⲞⲨⲀⲚ ⲞⲨⲚⲞϬ ⲚⲬⲓⲘⲰⲚ ⲚⲀⲰⲰⲠⲓ** recalls passages in Greek kalandologia, e.g. Vatic. gr. 1823 (ed. Wünsch, *BZ* 5 [1896] 419.7f) χειμὼν ἔσται μέγας καὶ ὑετώδης, ἀὴρ καθαρός. For μέγας in the sense of "long," see *LSJ* s.v. II 7. For **ⲚⲞϬ** cf. Eph. 6.3 (Thompson) **ⲚⲄⲢ ⲞⲨⲚⲞϬ ⲚⲞⲨⲞⲈⲓⲰ** (ἔση μακροχρόνιος).

18f **ⲚⲀⲎⲢ [ⲚⲀⲚ]ⲞⲨⲞⲨ**: cf. *CCAG* VII 126.9 ἀέρες καλοί. For **ⲀⲎⲢ** in the sense of "weather," see Reymond-Barns, *Coluthus* 148 n. 21 (ad 90 V ii 10 **ⲠⲓⲀⲎⲢ ⲈⲦⲚⲀⲚⲞⲨϤ**).

---

[1] Possibly to be added to the list is a passage from a Berlin text referred to below (ad V 3): on p. 56 we read **ⲠⲈⲪⲨⲤⲓⲞⲖⲞⲔⲞ[Ⲥ] ⲦⲀⲘⲀⲚ**. But elsewhere in the same text we find **ⲠⲈⲪⲨⲤⲓⲞⲖⲞⲔⲞⲤ ⲦⲀⲘ[Ⲁ] ⲘⲀⲚ** (p. 54) and **ⲠⲈⲪⲨⲤⲓⲞⲖⲰⲔⲞⲤ ⲦⲀⲘⲀ ⲘⲀⲚ** (p. 55). The first passage should therefore probably be corrected to **ⲠⲈⲪⲨⲤⲓⲞⲖⲞⲔⲞ[Ⲥ] ⲦⲀⲘⲀ ⟨ⲘⲀ⟩Ⲛ**.

V

2 [ⲚⲀⲚⲀⲬ]: restored on the basis of 12f ⲚⲀⲚⲀⲬ. For the phrase ⲚⲀⲬ ⲌⲎⲦⲞⲨ ⲂⲞⲖ (i.e. ⲚⲈⲬ, ⲈⲂⲞⲖ), see Crum, *Dict.* 642b.

3 [ⲚⲀ]ⲎⲀ]Ⲁ: for this section Till's *Bauernpraktik* (D V 2f) reads ⲚⲈⲤⲞⲨⲞ [ⲚⲀ]ⲎⲀ ⲚⲐⲈ ⲚⲠⲦⲀⲠⲈⲚ. The lacuna in the Michigan text is too long for ⲚⲀⲎⲀ, and I have restored, purely exempli-gratia, ⲚⲀⲎⲀⲀ. Unfortunately I have only one attestation for this form, and that uncertain: in *ZAeS* 33 (1895) 56, Erman published a Berlin text which contains the phrase ⲀⲦⲂⲰ ⲚⲈⲖⲀⲖⲈ ⲀⲤⲎⲀⲀⲈ ⲀⲤⲦⲀⲔⲀ, which I should prefer to articulate as ⲀⲤⲎⲀⲀ ⲈⲀⲤⲦⲀⲔⲀ. Other restorations, e.g., ⲚⲀⲎⲘⲀ (Crum, *Dict.* 565a), will not suit Till's text, and ⲎⲀ(Ⲗ), if it can be related to ⲎⲞⲞⲨⲈ ("be dry"), seems appropriate to the sense. If we have the common ⲎⲀ(Ⲗ), "rise" (for the form ⲎⲀⲀ, see Westendorf, *Handwörterbuch* 300), it does not appear to suit the context, since this verb regularly refers to the rising of the sun, etc. (Crum, *Dict.* 542b).

ⲦⲈⲠⲈⲚ: i.e. ⲦⲀⲠ(Ⲉ)Ⲛ, "cumin;" see Crum, *Dict.* 423a.

8 ⲚⲌⲀ ⲎⲰⲢⲠ: see Crum, *Dict.* 633a, who cites the Michigan text; cf. ⲌⲀ ⲢⲞⲨⲌⲈ below, lines 10 and 17.

9 ⲦⲈ: i.e. ⲚⲦⲈ; ⲦⲈ occurs in other texts written in vulgar Sahidic: see, e.g., Junker, *Koptische Poesie* I 411. ⲚⲦⲈ appears below, in line 16.

10 ⲞⲨⲚⲞϬ ⲚⲎⲎⲘ ⲠⲈ: ⲠⲈ here = "it means;" cf. Till's *Bauernpraktik* B V 11 ⲞⲨⲬⲒⲘⲰⲚ ⲈⲨⲌⲞⲞⲨ ⲠⲈ.

15 ⲞⲨⲀⲘⲚⲦ: i.e. ⲞⲨⲈⲘⲚⲦ, "a west wind." For the construction, see above, introd. p. 48. I cannot parallel this spelling of ⲈⲘⲚⲦ, but comparable is the alternation of ⲀⲘⲚⲦⲈ with ⲈⲘⲚⲦⲈ (Crum, *Dict.* 8b).

17f Till's *Bauernpraktik* offers no help at this point: D V 16 does not appear to correspond to the Michigan text. Tentatively, I suggest ⲞⲨⲀⲚ ⲞⲨⲚⲞϬ Ⲙ-Ⲡ[Ⲣ]Ⲱ ⲔⲚⲒ ⲚⲀ/[Ⲏ]ⲎⲠⲒ, "there will be a long winter of fatness." Ⲡ[Ⲣ]Ⲱ instead of ⲬⲒⲘⲰⲚ (above, R 17f) occurs in K 5506 R 10 (above, note to R 12f), ⲦⲈⲠⲢⲰ Ⲛ[Ⲁ]Ⲣ ⲔⲞⲨⲒ. If correctly restored, Ⲡ[Ⲣ]Ⲱ functions in the Michigan text as a status constructus. ⲔⲚⲒ I derive from ⲔⲚⲚⲈ, "be fat, sweet; fatness, sweetness" (Crum, *Dict.* 111b). The closest parallel seems to be the Bohairic ⲔⲈⲚⲒ (Crum, *ad loc.*); cf. also Subachmimic ⲔⲚⲒⲈ (Kasser, *Compléments*, ad 111b). I cannot parallel the use of ⲔⲚⲚⲈ with seasons; examination of the passages given in Crum shows that it is generally applied to crops and land. Metamorphical extensions, however, seem fairly common; to those given in Crum, add Orlandi, *S. Mercurio* 112.28, where it is related that a person died ⲌⲚ ⲞⲨⲘⲚⲦⲌⲀⲖⲞ ⲈⲤⲔⲒⲎⲞⲨ.

APPENDIX

Revision and reconstruction of TILL, *Bauernpraktik* E V 17 - D V 17. N. B. 1) Because of the extensive damage, I must emphasize the extremely hypothetical nature of some of the longer reconstructions; they should be taken only as exempli-gratia attempts to represent what the scribe might have written. 2) For my reversal of the sequence D E, see above, p. 51. 3) Till uses dots to mark letters damaged but certain as well as those which are uncertain. In my re-edition, I employ dots only when the reading is in doubt. For his use of the asterisk (*), see above, p. 49 n. 9.

```
E V    17 [COY COOY NTⲰBE NAI NE] NEMA
          [EIN EPϢAN ΠTHY NEIEBT EI EBOⲖ]
          [ΜΠEⲌOOY ETMMAY + 10        ]
D R       Π[E]ХIMⲰN OYNOϬ ΠE ΠϢM THY N̄
          THY NANOYOY N̄ΓΑΡΠΟС ETϢϢE NANO[Y]OY
          ΑⲖⲖΑ ⲌNKOYI NE· ΠΘENOΠEPON MN
          ΠEⲌMOM ...... [O]Y N̄ OYTA̲K̲[O NA]
       5  TAⲌE NECO[OY              NE]
          IⲰ NAAϢ[ΑI
          ΑⲖⲖΑ CEN[Α
          MN OYΠ[
          NAPX[ⲰN
      10  OYNⲌ[
          ———[
          EP[ϢAN ΠTHY NEIEBT EI EBOⲖ NCOY]
          CΑ[ϢЧ NTⲰBE              ]
          [.                       ]
          N[                       ]
      15  N[                       ]
          ———[
          E[PϢAN ΠTHY NEIEBT ϢⲰΠE NCOY]
          [ϢMOYN NTⲰBE            ]
D V       ΠM...... NAOYⲰ NETB[N]H NA
          NEХ ⲌHTOY EB[O]Ⲗ· NECOYO [NA]ϢΑ NΘE
          NΠTAΠEN· NPⲰME NAϢΠ ⲌNNOϬ
```

NϢϢNE· N[E]Ϣ[H]PE Ϣ[H]M NAMOY
5 [   ]..N.[
[EPϢAN OYTOY PHC EI EBOΛ N]2A ϢϢPN̄
[NCOY ΨIC NTϢBE NTE ΠT]HY NE
[M2IT EI EBOΛ 2A POY2E] OYNOϬ N
[ϢϢM ΠE NEKAPΠOC NAA]YΞAN[E]
10 [+ 5 NEKOYI NTBN]H NANX
[2HTOY EBOΛ   ]. ·AΛΛA
[MEYϢCK ΠEBIϢ NAEP Ϣ]AY NA
[   ]Ϣ·
[EPϢAN OYEMNT EI EBOΛ NC]OY
15 [MHT NTϢBE NTE ΠTOY PH]C EI
[EBOΛ 2A POY2E + 6]OY
[   ].

(*E V* 17) The sixth of Tubi: these are the signs. If the east wind comes forth on that day ... (*D R*) it means a great winter, the summer is moderate, the winds are good, the crops of the field are good but small, autumn and heat ... destruction will befall the sheep ... the asses will increase ... but they will ... with a ... the rulers ...

If the east wind comes forth on the seventh of Tubi ...

If the east wind comes on the eighth of Tubi ... (*D V*) ... the cattle will miscarry, the wheat will become as dry (?) as cumin, the men will suffer severe illnesses, the children will die ...

If a south wind comes forth on the dawn of the ninth of Tubi and the north (?) wind comes forth at evening, it means a great summer, the crops will increase ... the small livestock will miscarry ... but will not continue (to do so), the honey will become profitable ...

If a west wind comes forth on the tenth of Tubi and the south wind comes forth at evening ... a ...

E V

17-19 Till read].EMA in 17; to me the E seems certain, and it is preceded by what could be the right vertical of N. If NEMA/[EIN is correct, then we are dealing with some type of heading, perhaps similar to B V 9, the beginning of the first kalandologion: [MMAE]IN NCOY COOY [ET]ϢBE; cf. also F R 10, the end of this section: AYXϢK EBOΛ NϬI MMAEIN NCOY COOY ETϢϢBE. My restoration is, of course, purely exempli gratia.

Till marks 17 as "letzte Zeile?" But the photograph shows nothing that has to be interpreted as the original lower margin, and B V, which preserves the margin, has 19 lines (cf. *Bauernpraktik*, Nachtrag 176).[1] The reconstruction of 18 and 19

[1] Till here edits a Vienna fragment, K 4858, which preserves the end of B V. The

is based upon Mich. R 6-8, which I associate with 6 Tubi (see above, note to Mich. R 3).

18 NЄIЄBT: this word appears in TILL's *Bauernpraktik* once as HBT (F R 3), and once as ЄIHϤT (F V 3). The Michigan text offers yet different spellings (see note to R 6f). In the face of this diversity I have preferred to restore the common ЄIЄBT throughout, rather than to guess at what the scribe may have actually written.

19 The lacuna at the end of the line might have held, e.g., NANOY ΠMOOY (cf. Mich. R 8).

D R

1 Π[Є]ХIMШN: ΠШ...MШN stands in Till's text, and the latter writes in his note ad loc.: "MШ sehr unsicher; Π[Є]Х[ЄI]MШN scheint möglich." Unless the photograph is deceptive, Π[Є]ХIMШN appears inevitable: it is quite similar to ХIMШN in E V 7 (where Till's text should read OYN OYNO]б NХIMШN NAШШΠЄ).

2 NANOYOY: Till read NA.(?)OY, and in his note added: "wohl NANOYOY." The reading appears certain from the photograph.

ШШϤЄ: i.e. CШϤЄ; see Till ad loc., and cf. Mich. R 13f NЄKAPΠOC NTCШϤЄ.

NANO[Y]OY: Till read NANOY. in his text, and wrote in his note: "OY steht über dem zweiten N; wohl NAN[OY]OY." The photograph reveals traces of the first O.

4f For these lines Till read:

ΠЄ2MOM .... OYTA.[..(.)
TA2Є NЄCO[

I believe that [O]YN̄ OYTAK[O NA]TA2Є NЄCO[OY suits both the traces — K seems certain — and the sense (cf. e.g. *CCAG* X 152.28 θάνατος ... προβάτων), but I cannot decipher what immediately follows ΠЄ2MOM. The 3rd letter is either Ϥ, Ш or M, and the 5th and 6th may be ΠЄ. NAШШΠЄ is paleographically possible — though Ш is hard to discern — but it yields little meaning. The phrase ΠθЄNOΠЄPON (= φθι-νόπωρον) MN ΠЄ2MOM occurs also in E V 9 and probably in E R 14f, but the context is too fragmentary to be of help. The collocation suggests that ΠЄ2MOM refers to a season, but I cannot parallel the word with such a significance; if it does refer to a season, it may be the hot period following autumn.

6 IШ NAAϤ[AI: suggested by Crum (see TILL, *Bemerkungen* 328). I have added NЄ at the end of the preceding line.

7 A[Λ]ΛA CЄN[A Till.

11-15 In 11f Till read ЄP[ϤANCOY COOY ЄTШBЄ ХШШϤЄ]/.[, because he believed that he was dealing with the type of kalandologion which started in B V 10 (see above, p. 46). Lines 11-15 may have been similar to Mich. R 8-14 (see note to Mich. R 3), although the material in the predictions would have had to be some-

first line contains part of B V 15, four additional lines follow, and then Till marks "Rand."

what more extensive in the latter.   The present section, after **TⲰBE**, could probably hold no more than 80 letters, and the corresponding Michigan lines have 109.

15 **N[**: **.[** Till.

16 **E[PϢAN**: **.[** Till.   The **E**, though damaged, appears certain.   It extends well into the left margin, thereby indicating a new section, and the beginning of the horizontal line marking off sections can be seen above it.   From line 16 to D V 4 there is at least partial correspondence with Mich. R 15 - V 6.

D V

1-5 These lines appear in Till as follows:

    ⲠM......NAOYⲰN. **[**   **]** **..A**

    NEⲭT..O.E...(.) **OYN[..]MAⲖEⲐE**

    NTTA.... **NPⲰME** **NA[MOY(?)** **ZE]NNOϬ**

    NϢⲰNE **N[AϢⲰⲠE**   **]OY**

               ].N[

The Michigan text (V 1-6) provides assistance in deciphering lines 1-4, but the first part of line 1 corresponds to nothing in Mich. and I have been unable to go beyond Till's text. **ⲠMOOY ⲠETNAOYⲰ**, "the water will cease," is just barely possible. In line 1, there is no room for **NETBNOOYE**, which occurs in Mich. V 1; **NETB[N]H** at least fits the exiguous traces (cf. below, line 10 **NTBN]H**).   On **[NA]ϢA** in line 2, see the note on Mich. V 3.   The Michigan text offers no help in restoring line 5.

6-13 Till read:

        ] **.ⲰPⲚ**

           ].

           ] **...**

        AY]ⲌAN

        ]ⲠNANA²

        ]. **·AⲖⲖA**

          ]Ⲱ.

(Note that a line was accidentally omitted in Till's transcript between 11 and 13.) For this section, the reconstruction is modeled on Mich.   V 7-14, but here again correspondence between the two texts is not exact.   The end of line 7 is partic-

---

² Till ad loc.: "**A** oder **ⲭ**."

ularly difficult to decipher, and possibly there is reference to some other wind.]H in 10 seems secure; hence probably **TBNH** was written, not **TBNOOYE** as in Mich. V 12. Possibly **ΛYⲰ ON** stood at the beginning of 10. Nothing in Mich. assists in reconstructing 13.

14-17 Till has:[3]

]··

]CN

]OY

The **N** of **CN** is by no means certain, and under magnification **EI** emerges as a distinct alternative; if correct, it is ideally suited to the restoration, which is modeled on Mich. V 15-17. The end of 16 does not appear to correspond to anything in the Michigan text, unless **OY** continues with **NOϬ** (as in Mich. V 18); if so, the scribe would probably have increased the size of the preceding letters in the line. Of line 17, a tiny trace of ink, no longer decipherable, remains. There may have been room for one other line below 17 (cf. above, note to E V 17-19).

[3] Till marks as line 13 ( ]) what is in fact the space between the two sections.

INDICES

(N.B. In these indices, I omit Nos. 1, 3-5, 7 and 8, which duplicate, except for a few variant readings, Biblical texts already known in Coptic; for the variants, the reader is referred to the apparatus accompanying each text. For No. 6, I list only those words which survive at least in part and I disregard those proposed in my exempli-gratia reconstruction.)

I

INDEX OF PROPER NAMES

INDEX OF COPTIC WORDS

ⲀⲚ 9 V i 6
ⲀⲚⲞⲔ 9 V ii 5; 10 R 11; 11 R 7
ⲀⲚⲞⲚ 9 R i 22
ⲀⲠⲀ See index of proper names
ⲀⲠⲈ 10 V 16 (ⲀⲠⲎ)
ⲀⲦ-
    ⲀⲦⲬⲀ ⲢⲰϤ 2 V 5
    ⲘⲈⲦⲀⲦⲚⲈⲒ 2 R 3
ⲀⲨⲰ 9 R i 19, 23, V i 1; 12.14; 13 R 8
ⲀϢ ⲀⲌⲞⲘ 2 V 4

Ⲉ- 2 V 7; 6 R 7, V 8 (both Ⲁ-); 9 R i 6, 17, 21, 24, 32, ii 2, 12, 17, 21, 29,
    34, V i 1, 4; 10 R 4, 7, 10, 11, V 8, 14? (see note ad loc.); 12.11; 13 R 5
    ⲈⲢⲞ= 9 R i 33, ii 33; 10 R 18, 20, 21, V 19
    See also ⲈⲂⲞⲖ, ⲈⲌⲞⲨⲚ, ⲈⲌⲢⲀ=, ⲈⲬⲚ-, ⲌⲢⲀⲒ
ⲈⲂⲒϢ 13 R 12, V 14
ⲈⲂⲞⲖ 2 V 10; 6 R 10, V 11 (both ⲀⲂⲀⲖ); 9 R i 31, ii 18, 25; 10 R 8, 12, 13,
    V 9; 13 R 7, V 2 (ⲂⲞⲖ), 7, 9, 13 (ⲂⲞⲖ), 15, 17
ⲈⲘⲚⲦ 13 V 15 (ⲀⲘⲚⲦ)
ⲈⲚⲈⲌ
    ϢⲀ Ⲉ. 10 R 13
ⲈⲢⲎⲨ 6 V 8
ⲈⳘⲦ
    ⲘⲠⲈⳘⲦ 10 R 1 (ⲌⲈⲠ.)
ⲈⲦⲂⲈ- 9 R i 20; 10 V 3; 13 R 4
ⲈⲌⲞⲨⲚ 9 R ii 32
ⲈⲌⲢⲀ= 11 V 6 (see note ad loc.)
ⲈⲬⲚ- 9 R ii 1, 3
    ⲈⲬⲰ= 10 R 8

ⲎⲒ 2 R 7

ЄI   13 R 7, V 7, 9, 15, 17
ЄIЄBT   13 R 6 (ΛЄBT), 15 (ΛHBT)
ЄIMЄ   2 R 6 (ЄIMI; see note ad loc.)
ЄIPЄ   2 R 11 (ЄIPI; see note ad loc.); 9 R i 14, ii 5, 20, 33; 10 R 17, 21
    ЄP KOYI   13 R 13
    ЄP MΛCTIΓOIN   2 R 4
    P NOЧPЄ   13 R 5 (NOBPI)
    P ΦΘONI   6 V 8
    ЄP ШBHP   2 V 7
    ЄP ШΛY   13 V 14
    P 2ШB   9 R i 13
    P 2OTЄ   10 R 4, 12
    P 6Λ(O)YΛN   6 R 8
ЄIШT   9 R i 27; 10 V 8

KЄ   2 R 10; 9 R ii 34, V i 11; 10 V 22
KOYI   13 V 12
    ЄP KOYI   13 R 13
KШ   2 V 5 (XΛ-); 9 R i 30, ii 23; 10 R 8, 22, V 5
KNNЄ   13 V 18 (KNI; see note ad 13 V 17f)
KΛC   2 V 9 (KЄC)
KШTЄ   10 R 4, 7, 15
KΛ2   2 R 8 (KЄ2I); 10 V 2; 13 R 9

MOY   vb. 2 R 7 (MШOYT⁺); 13 V 6
   nn. 2 R 7; 9 R i 17
MOYI   10 R 2
MKΛ2   2 R 5 (ЄMKЄ2)
MMIN MMO=   9 R ii 4, 9
MN-   with 2 V 8, 9 (both NЄM); 10 R 18, V 4 (both MЄ), 9, 22 (MЄ)
    NMMΛ=   9 R i 26
MN-   there is not 6 V 3
MOYN   vb. 10 R 13
   nn. 9 R i 31
MINЄ
    NTЄIMINЄ   6 V 10
MOYNK   2 R 6 (MΛNK=)
MNNCШ=   9 R ii 19
MNT-
    MЄTΛTNЄI   2 R 3
    MNTПЄTNΛNOYЧ   6 V 2
    MNT X̄C̄   6 V 2

ⲚⲞⲨϪⲈ   10 R 18, V 19
   ⲚⲈϪ ⲒϨⲦ= ⲈⲂⲞⲖ 13 V 2, 13 (both ⲚⲀϪ, ⲂⲞⲖ)
ⲚⲞϬ   9 R i 6, 19, 28, ii 11, V i 3; 10 R 16, V 8, 11; 13 R 17, V 4, 10, 18
ⲚϬⲒ   2 R 6, V 3 (both ⲚϪⲈ? See note ad 2 R 6f); 9 R i 2, 27; 12.14 (ⲈϬⲒ)

ⲞⲚ   9 V i 11; 10 R 3, 9, 14, V 7, 20

ⲠⲒ- Ⲧ- Ⲛ-   defin. art., passim
   ⲠⲒ-   2 V 7, 8; 11 V 5
ⲠⲀ- ⲦⲀ- ⲚⲀ-   poss. pron., passim
ⲠⲀ- ⲦⲀ- ⲚⲀ-   poss. art. 6 V 4; 10 R 20, V 2
ⲠⲀⲒ ⲦⲀⲒ ⲚⲀⲒ   6 V 10 (ⲠⲈⲒ); 9 R ii 6, 20, 22, 31, V i 2, 7, ii 7; 10 V 11; 13 R 3
   ⲠⲈⲒ- ⲦⲈⲒ- ⲚⲈⲒ-   2 R 11; 9 R i 11, 12, 13, V i 4, 9, ii 4; 10 R 7 (ⲠⲒ), V 8,
   10; 11 R 7 (ⲠⲀⲒ)
ⲠⲈ   heaven   10 R 10, V 2
ⲠⲈ   copula   2 R 8; 9 R i 10, ii 22, V i 2, 3, ii 7; 10 R 16, 19, V 1, 10? (see note
   ad loc.), 11; 13 R 3, V 10
ⲠⲢⲰ   13 V 18
ⲠⲀⲢⲘϨⲞⲦⲠ   13 R 1, 2 (both ⲠⲀⲢⲘϨⲀⲦ)
ⲠⲰⲢϢ   10 V 9
ⲠⲰⲦ   10 R 1
ⲠⲰϨ[6 R 3 (see note ad loc.)
ⲠⲈϪⲈ-   10 R 5, V 10

ⲢⲞ
   ⲔⲀ ⲢⲰ=   2 V 5 (ϪⲀ)
   ⲔⲰ ϨⲀⲢⲰ=   9 R i 30
ⲢⲰⲘⲈ   9 V i 5, 9, ii 5; 13 V 4
   ⲢⲘⲚϨⲎⲦ   10 R 19 (ⲢⲈⲘⲈϨⲎⲦ)
ⲢⲀⲚ   10 R 11, 20, V 21
ⲢⲎⲤ   13 V 7, 17
ⲢⲎ†
   ⲘⲠⲀⲒⲢⲎ†   11 R 7
ⲢⲞⲞⲨϢ   10 R 18, V 19
ⲢⲀϢⲈ   vb.   9 R i 34, ii 3; 10 V 9
   nn.   6 V 1 (ⲢⲈϢⲈ); 10 V 9
ⲢⲞⲨϨⲈ   13 V 10, 17

ⲤⲀ   10 V 14
ⲤⲂⲂⲈ   6 R 1
ⲤⲞⲂⲦⲈ   6 V 10
ⲤⲞⲖⲤⲖ   10 V 13

CON 6 R 6
COΠC 10 R 7, 17, 23, V 5, 11, 17
CⲰTM 9 R i 23
CⲰTΠ 10 V 3 (CⲰΠT sic)
CHY
    COY- 13 R 3, 16, V 8, 15
COYO 13 V 2 (COYⲀ)
COOYTN 9 R ii 32
CⲰⲨE 13 R 14
CⲌⲀI 12.11

TⲀ(Є)IO vb. 10 V 5
    ⲨOY TⲀIO 10 R 21
    nn. 9 V i 4, 8, ii 4, 12 (?)
+ 9 R ii 8; 10 V 4
    + OYⲨ 13 R 12
TⲰBE 13 R 3, 16, V 8, 16
TBNH 13 R 10 (TBNAYE), V 1, 12
TⲰBⲌ 2 R 10
TAKO 13 R 14
TEⲖHⲖ 10 V 3
TAMO 10 V 10; 13 R 4
TONTN 10 R 20
TAΠ(Є)N 13 V 3 (TEΠEN)
THP= 2 R 8; 6 R 9; 9 R ii 27; 10 V 2; 13 R 9
TOOT= See ⲌIOYE
THY 13 R 6, 15, V 9
    TOY- 13 V 7, 16
TOOY 10 V 1
TⲀ(O)YO 9 R i 2, 11; 10 V 21
TOYNOC 9 V ii 1
TOYⲬO 10 R 2
TⲰⲨ 2 R 5 (TAⲨ=)
TAⲨE OEIⲨ 6 R 1 (ⲀEIⲨ)
TAⲌO 2 V 3; 10 R 3
TⲰⲌM 6 R 5 (TⲀⲌM-)

OY- indef. art., passim
    OY- ... NOYⲰT 9 R ii 23
OY what? 9 V ii 3; 10 V 10? (see note ad loc.)
OYⲀ 2 R 11 (OYEI); 9 R ii 2, 16

OYШ
   + OYШ 13 R 12
OYN- 2 R 9 (OYON); 10 R 15 (OYΛN); 13 R 17, V 17 (both OYΛN)
OYNΛM 10 R 22, V 17
OYNOY
   TENOY 9 R ii 10; 11 V 1 (+NOY)
OYNOЧ 10 V 2
OYШNϨ 9 R ii 17
OYOП 11 V 7 (OYΛB+); 12.1
   ПETOYΛΛB 9 R i 2
OYШCЧ 6 R 3
OYШT
   OY- ... NOYШT 9 R ii 23
OYШTB 9 V i 2
OYOEIШ 9 R i 25
   NOY. NIM 10 V 18
OYШϢ 9 R ii 16
OYШϨ 2 V 5
OYШϨM 10 R 3, 19, V 1, 13 (all П̄O̅Y̅)

ШNϨ vb. 10 R 16, 17, 21, V 12; 13 R 10 (ШNΛϨ)
   nn. 9 V i 12
ШCK 13 V 14
ШϢ 2 V 6; 10 R 12

Ϣ- 9 V ii 8
   ϢϬOM 2 R 9 (ⳢOM)
ϢΛ- 10 R 1, 13
ϢΛΛ 13 V 3 (see note ad loc.)
ϢHI 10 R 2
ϢI 9 R ii 21
ϢBHP 9 R i 10
   EP Ϣ. 2 V 7
   Ϣ. P ϨШB 9 R i 13
   Ϣ. NΛEITOYPГOC 10 V 22 (EΛIT.)
ϢHM
   ϢHPE Ϣ. 13 V 5
ϢШM 13 V 10
ϢШNE 13 V 5
ϢШП 13 V 4
ϢШПE 2 V 4 (ϢШПI); 6 R 7 (ϨШПE); 9 R i 25; 12.13, 15; 13 R 6, 16, 18 (all
   three ϢШПI)

ϢΠΗΡΕ 10 V 8
ϢΑΑΡ 2 V 9 (ϢΕΡ)
ϢΗΡΕ 10 R 18, V 11; 12.4
   Ϣ. ϢΗΜ 13 V 5
ϢϢΡΠ 13 V 8
   ΝϢΟΡΠ 9 R ii 33
ϢΤΟΡΤΡ 6 R 4 (ϢΤΑΡΤ[Ρ(Ε)†)
ϢΑΥ
   Ρ ϢΑΥ 13 V 14
   ϢΟΥ ΤΑΙΟ 10 R 21
ϢΟΥΟ 6 V 7
ϢΟΥϢΟΥ 10 V 5
ϢΑΧΕ vb. 9 R i 33; V i 3
   nn. 9 introd., R ii 1, 4, 18, V i 1, ii 2, 9; 12.11, 14, 15

ϤΙ
   ϤΑΙ ϢΜΝΟΥϤΕ 10 V 23 (ϢΕΝΟΥΒΕ)

ϨΑ- 10 R 23, V 6, 12, 18; 13 V 8 (ΝϨΑ), 10, 17
   ϨΑΡϢ= 9 R i 30
ϨΑΕ 13 R 13 (ΘΑΗ)
ϨΕ 9 R ii 2; 13 R 4 (ΘΗ)
   ΝΘΕ 9 R ii 27; 13 V 3 (ΘΗ)
   ΝΤΕΙϨΕ 2 R 11 (ϨΗ)
   ΤΑΙ ΤΕ ΘΕ 9 V i 2
ϨΗ-, ϨΗΤ= fore part
   Ρ ϨΟΤΕ ϨΗΤ= 10 R 4, 12 (both ΝϨΗΤ=)
ϨΗ-, ϨΗΤ= belly
   ΝΕΧ ϨΗΤ= ΕΒΟΛ 13 V 2, 13 (both ΝΑΧ, ΒΟΛ)
ϨΙ- 10 R 22, V 17
   See also ϨΙΤΝ-, ϨΙΧΝ-
ϨΟ 13 R 9
ϨϢϢ= 9 R i 22
ϨϢΒ 9 V i 3; 10 V 10
   ϢΒΗΡ Ρ Ϩ. 9 R i 13
ϨΛΟϬ vb. 10 V 21
   nn. 10 V 14
ϨΑΜΟΙ 2 R 8
ϨΝ- 2 R 2, 3, 5 (all three ϨΕΝ), V 1? (see note ad 2 V 1-3), 4, 6 (both ϨΕΝ); 6
   R 10, V 9 (both ϨΝ); 9 R i 25, 26, 30, ii 18, 26, V ii 2, 11?; 10 R 10 (ϨΕ);
   V 8 (Ν; see note ad loc.), 14, 16 (both ϨΕ); 11 R 3, 5, V 3 (all three ϨΕΝ);
   12.13; 13 R 1, 2? (both ϨΙ; see note ad 13 R 1f)
   ΝϨΗΤ= 10 R 16 (ΕΝϨΗΤ=)

ϨⲢⲀⲒ upper part
 ⲈϨⲢⲀⲒ 2 V 7 (ⲈϨⲢⲎⲒ); 9 V ii 2
ϨⲎⲦ, ϨⲦⲎ=
 ⲘⲔⲀϨ ⲚϨⲎⲦ 2 R 5 (ⲈⲘⲔⲈϨ)
 ⲠⲘⲚϨⲎⲦ 10 R 19 (ⲢⲈⲘⲈϨⲎⲦ)
 ⲰⲀⲚⲀϨⲦⲎ= 10 R 22, V 18
ϨⲞⲦⲈ
 Ⲣ ϨⲞⲦⲈ 10 R 4, 12
ϨⲰⲦⲂ 2 R 10 (ϨⲀⲦⲂⲈ=; see note ad loc.)
ϨⲒⲦⲚ- 9 V ii 3
ϨⲎⲨ 9 R i 24
ϨⲞⲞⲨ day 2 V 2, 3; 13 R 7
 ⲘⲠⲞⲞⲨ 10 V 9 (ⲈⲠ.)
ϨⲞⲞⲨ bad 2 V 3 (ϨⲀⲞⲨ)
 ⲠⲈⲐⲞⲞⲨ 10 R 3
ϨⲒⲞⲨⲈ
 ϨⲒ ⲦⲞⲞⲦ= 12.10
ϨⲞⲨⲞ
 ⲚϨⲞⲨⲞ 9 R ii 1
ϨⲞⲨⲈⲒⲦ
 ϨⲞⲨⲈⲒⲦⲈ 12.13 (ϨⲞⲨⲒⲦⲈ)
ϨⲀϨ 9 R i 31; 12.10
ϨⲒⲬⲚ- 10 V 15 (ϨⲒⲬⲈ)

ⲬⲈ 2 R 6; 9 R ii 31; 10 R 11, 12, 13, 17, 18, V 3, 6, 10, 12, 17, 18, 19
ⲬⲒ 13 R 9
ⲬⲈⲔⲀⳞ 9 R ii 8
ⲬⲰⲰⲘⲈ 12.3
ⲬⲠⲞ 12.3
ⲬⲰⲰⲢⲈ vb. 2 R 3 (ⲬⲀⲢ⳦)
 nn. 10 R 10
ⲬⲢⲞ 10 V 4
ⲬⲞ(Ⲉ)ⲒⳞ 10 R 4, 13, V 3 (all three ⲞⳞ̄)
ⲬⲒⳞⲈ 9 introd.; 10 V 1
ⲬⲞⲨϤ 13 R 2 (ⲬⲰϤ)
ⲬⲰ(Ⲱ)ϬⲈ 2 V 10 (ⲬⲰⲬⲒ; see note ad loc.)

ϬⲞⲘ 9 R ii 18; 10 R 13, V 4
 ⲰϬⲞⲘ 2 R 9 (ⲬⲞⲘ)
ϬⲰⲘ 13 R 11
ϬⲢⲎⲠⲈ 10 V 15
ϬⲀ(Ⲩ)ⲞⲚ
 Ⲣ Ϭ. 6 R 8 (ϬⲀ[(Ⲟ)ⲨⲀⲚ)

ϭⲱⲩⲧ   9 R ii 21, 29
ϭⲓⲭ   2 R 2 (ⲭⲓⲭ); 10 V 16

Doubtful (see notes ad locc.)
] .ⲱⲱⲥ   6 V 9
] .ⲋⲛⲉⲥⲉⲙ[6 V 6

III

INDEX OF GREEK WORDS

ϹΥΠΟΘΕϹΙϹ   9 R i 32, ii 11, 23, 26

ΦΘΟΝΕΙ
   P Φ.   6 V 8 (-ΝΙ)

ΧΑΙΡΕ   10 V 13 (ΧΕΡΕ)
ΧΕΙΜΩΝ   13 R 17 (ΧΙ-)
ΧΡΕΟϹ   9 V ii 6, 10 (both -ΩϹ)

ΨΥΧΗ   9 R i 24

ϹΩϹ   9 R ii 10, 33

PLATES

No. 2 R No. 2 V

No. 6 R No. 6 V

No. 11 R

No. 11 V

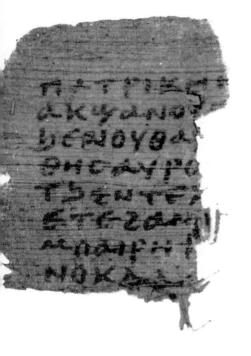